Praise for *The Other Talk*

"This book not only identifies the many issues that should be addressed well before they come up, it also makes the entire topic of planning for later-life issues seem less daunting and unsettling than one might expect. It feels not only doable but positive. You *can* create the end-of-life picture you want—if you address it head on and early with the ones you love."

—George, editor

"This is a book everyone should read, especially because it's a subject we all just want to avoid. It's a great catalyst and road map to get my family and me talking about the things that will really matter down the road."

—Andrea, mother with two adult daughters

"I can't recommend this book highly enough. I read it as part of my job, and I was blown away with its succinct, powerful, important information. If everyone would read this book and follow its advice, millions of adult children would spend less time frantically making decisions, worrying about the future, not knowing what to do. Buy this and read it!"

—John, healthcare practitioner

"I really appreciated the straightforward style of *The Other Talk*. Tim Prosch's clear advice on how we older baby boomers can prevent burdens to our children is incredibly helpful and a good reminder to not wait too long before we have this 'other' talk."

—Susan, teacher

"I'm buying copies of this book for each of my three kids and planning to start the Other Talk over the holidays. We can't afford to wait!"

—Julie, mother of three adult children

The
Other™
Talk

A Guide to Talking with Your Adult
Children About the Rest of Your Life

TIM PROSCH

New York Chicago San Francisco Athens London Madrid
Mexico City Milan New Delhi Singapore Sydney Toronto

A previous edition of this book was published in 2012 by Contact Points. It is now out of print.

3 4 5 6 7 8 9 0   QFR/QFR   1 9 8 7 6 5 4

ISBN   978-0-07-183098-0
MHID   0-07-183098-7

e-ISBN   978-0-07-182967-0
e-MHID   0-07-182967-9

Library of Congress Cataloging-in-Publication Data
Prosch, Timothy.
  The other talk: a guide to talking with your adult children about the rest of your life /
    Tim Prosch. pages cm
  Includes bibliographic references.
  ISBN-13: 978-0-07-183098-0 (pbk. : alk. paper)
  ISBN-10: 0-07-183098-7 (alk. paper)
  1. Aging parents—Family relationships. 2. Aging parents—Care. 3. Adult children of
aging parents—Family relationships. I. Title.
HQ1063.6.P76 2013
305.26—dc23   2013029111

The Other Talk is dedicated to my daughter, Dakota, her husband, Fernando, and my grandson, Gabe.

Contents

PART THREE

Turning the Other Talk into an Action Plan

Acknowledgments

A number of people are responsible for the book you have
in your hands:

Tom Miller, Executive Editor, McGraw-Hill Professional;
Jodi Lipson, Director, AARP Book Division; and Corinne
Hayward, AARP Editorial Researcher, who made a good
manuscript better

Lauren Wittig, a seasoned author, who helped guide me
through the byzantine workings of today's publishing world

Sam Winstanley, who helped design and direct the development of the website www.theothertalk.com along with
Tasty, Inc.

Elaine Gloeckle, who has been my favorite art director for
many years

My many friends who were willing to share their personal
stories about life before the Other Talk

Most importantly, my wife, Pam, who not only kept me motivated and energized about this book for seven long years but also played a very important role in editing the manuscript and believing in the concept

About This Book

One of the most important conversations you have with your children is what is euphemistically called "the Talk," the one about the birds and the bees. But there is another equally critical time in your kids' lives when you need to sit them down to talk about the facts of life.

I call it "the Other Talk." This time it's not about the beginning of life. It's about your last years of life and the issues and decisions and role reversals that you and your family need to confront while you are still able to lead the conversation.

The Other Talk is designed to help you get past the many emotional barriers that can exist between you and your family, putting you on the road to an open, honest dialogue about the four essentials for the rest of your life:

1. Financing your uncertain future
2. Selecting the best living arrangements

3. Getting the medical care you need
4. Taking charge at the end of your life

Start reading this book today so you can begin preparing for one of the most important conversations your family will ever have.

Introduction

Among today's books, whether on actual or virtual shelves, you'll find many titles that provide tips and techniques on how to care for and cope with an aging and ultimately dying parent.

Typically, these self-help books are designed to assist adult children who have been confronted by unexpected crises that disrupt their parents' lives: physical, such as a broken hip or a diagnosis of life-threatening illness; financial, such as a sudden spike in medical expenses or unexpected decline in net worth; or psychological, such as the emergence of mental illness or the onslaught of dementia.

The problem is that these books focus on what adult children should do after a parental crisis hits. While this reactive approach is necessary in coping with the challenges that occur in front of you, it is built on the assumption that the crisis is the children's cross to bear and that the parents have become innocent bystanders. Further, this problem-solution mindset ignores the long-term emotional consequences that can subvert both sides of the family relationship.

On the one hand, adult children can become overwhelmed by the depth and breadth of responsibilities and the emotional stress of guessing—and being second-guessed about—what their parents would want done in a given situation. On the other hand, their aging parents' last years can be made miserable by the resentments associated with their loss of control over day-to-day living and their feelings of embarrassment and failure at becoming a burden on their kids.

Preempt the Crisis

The Other Talk takes the polar opposite approach from all those books that tell adult children how to cope with failing, incompetent parents.

First, it places the responsibility for taking action directly in your hands. It's important that you—the parents, not the kids—handle this. By adopting this preemptive, collaborative mindset, you will actually empower every member of your family (you as well as your children) for the events that lie ahead.

Second, it takes a proactive approach by helping you prepare for the various decisions and actions that will eventually need to be taken, rather than waiting for the next unexpected (although often predictable) crisis to envelop your family.

Clearly, no one knows how the last sentence of one's life will be written—how and when declining health and death will occur. But we all know with a fair amount of certainty what issues will arise and the decisions that will need to be made.

I believe the answer is that parents need to take the initiative to have what I call "the Other Talk" with their kids. While they are still physically and mentally able to lead that discussion, parents need to sit the family down and walk through the four essentials:

1. Financing your uncertain future. How do you budget for unknown needs and an uncertain length of time?

2. Selecting the best living arrangements. Will you, and if so when will you, move out of your home to some form of assisted living?

3. Getting the medical care you need. Who will advocate for your medical needs, and how?

4. Taking charge at the end of your life. How do you want your kids to start taking over decision making when you no longer can?

The ultimate goal here is to provide you with the tools and a road map to successfully engage your own kids in the Other Talk. First, I'll help you overcome the emotional hurdles that will present themselves when you address your eventual demise and explore the role reversal that you and your kids will experience. Second, I'll provide concepts and techniques that will help you and your family thoroughly understand and prepare for the facts of life for this stage of your life.

Why I Wrote This Book

Throughout my career as a marketing manager, I have focused my energies and attention on understanding and addressing the needs, wants, and challenges of the baby boom generation—my generation—for a variety of national and international organizations.

In the past 15 years while I have been running a strategic marketing consultancy, I have honed in on eldercare and end-of-life issues. What drove me to write this book?

1. The hundreds of interviews I conducted with people who are (like me) currently in their fifties and sixties to determine the perceptions, attitudes, and mindset that this unique generation brings to the various decisions at the end of life. One clear message was that we do not want our kids to suffer through the same frustrations, arguments, and unpleasant surprises that we experienced with our parents.

2. The tug-of-war in 2005 between Terri Schiavo's husband and her parents over what she wanted done at the end of her life.

3. The rapidly declining health of my own parents, and along with it, the escalating frustrations and financial crises created by our family's lack of communication.

4. A "perfect storm" that has been brewing in geriatric care in recent years, scheduled to hit us just as we reach 65:

- **More people.** The 65-and-older population will grow more than 60 percent between now and 2025.
- **Longer lives.** Today's 65-year-olds will likely live, on average, for another 18.5 years.
- **Fewer medical professionals.** The supply of internists, geriatric doctors, and nurses is declining.

You and your kids need to start preparing. You should have the Other Talk now, and then you need to keep on talking. This book is the catalyst that can get you there.

PART ONE

Why Have the Other Talk?

Talking about it puts my family in an uncomfortable situation. . . . It's best left unsaid.

—Sally, research respondent

People just won't think about or talk about
their long-term future. It took me five years
to get my in-laws to start planning, and I
sell insurance for a living.

—Chad, insurance agent

CHAPTER ONE

Defining the Dimensions of the Other Talk

I'll never put my kids through what just happened to me with my parents!

—Several focus group participants

Do you remember how difficult—and absolutely necessary—it was when it came time to sit with your kids to have "the Talk," the one about the birds and the bees? If you are anything like me, your initial reaction was to procrastinate, to keep the door firmly closed on any conversations that revolved around orgasms and vaginas and penises with your kid (in my case, a 12-year-old daughter).

But why would I even consider putting off a conversation that was so critical to the future well-being of my child? There were three reasons:

1. **It was an emotionally challenging subject.** It was uncomfortable and embarrassing to sit down with my daughter to explain how the body parts interact and what the physical sensations would be.

2. **It acknowledged an inevitable transformation that I didn't want to face.** If we didn't have the Talk, I could hold on just a little longer to my fantasy that my little girl, my bouncy, energetic, wide-eyed, giggly preteen, would remain just that . . . forever.

3. **I wanted to maintain the existing parent-child relationship.** I could pretend that our relationship would never change. We'd still read the Sunday comics on the couch, I'd still help her with her homework, and I wouldn't have to contemplate some boy mauling her (or, God forbid, vice versa) in the backseat of his car.

Because of the anticipated discomfort for me, my wife, and my daughter, I even contemplated the sex-talk drive-by, where I would drop off the brochures on her bed with the note, "Let me know if you have any questions." As a result, I could stay hidden behind "the birds and the bees" euphemism and avoid any real semblance of a two-way dialogue.

Ultimately, I decided not to procrastinate anymore, and I stepped up to that Talk—I recognized that there were potential life-altering consequences to putting it off indefinitely:

unexpected pregnancy, sexual disease, and unfulfilling relationships with the opposite sex, to name a few.

Of course, that first Talk isn't just about plumbing issues, like where things go, how things work, and how embryos turn into babies. It's also about the judgments and decisions that need to be made as our children enter an important new phase in their lives.

Initially, the Talk was uncomfortable for all of us, but as the first conversation unfolded and subsequent ones ensued, we began to realize that we were empowering our daughter for something that would have far-reaching and ongoing consequences for the rest of her life.

The Other Talk

There is another equally critical time in your kids' lives when you need to sit them down to talk about the facts of life—discomfort notwithstanding. This time it's not about the beginning of life or how babies are made. It's about the end of life—yours—and the many issues and decisions that will confront you and your children.

It's the *Other* Talk.

Unfortunately, if you're anything like the hundreds of families and medical personnel and end-of-life practitioners whom I've interviewed in preparation for this book, you will most likely put off indefinitely any substantive discussion with your kids about what they might expect in your last years. In fact, most parents *never* have the Other Talk. The National Hospice Foundation has found that 75 percent of Americans don't make their end-of-life decisions known to their families through either verbal or written communication.

Furthermore, only 55 percent of adult children have talked to their parents about what to do if the parents can't live independently, according to a 2009 Pew Research Center survey. Some children avoid this most intimate of conversations because they believe their parents don't want to talk about it. Others think they know what their parents want. And some simply don't want to face the very real truth that old age will most likely include disease, injury, frailty, and even loneliness and depression.

Why Do Most Americans Keep the Door Firmly Closed on the Other Talk?

It turns out that the thoughts are remarkably similar to those that stand in the way of "the birds and the bees" talk.

It's an Emotionally Challenging Subject

Sitting down with your kids to talk about your later years can be uncomfortable, painful, depressing, even paralyzing, especially when you come to the part about the various stages of your deterioration, mentally and physically, and, of course, that last sentence: The end.

I found that to avoid stirring up these scary emotions, many of the parents I interviewed for this book had taken a protective stance: I don't want to put my family in a state of depression and panic by talking about it.

Not surprisingly, the reality is that this "sweep it under the rug" attitude usually has as much to do with the mental fragility of the parent as it does with that of the children. It seems the longer we can cling to the previous phase of our lives (the one where we are healthy, independent, and care-free), the less we need to deal with the final one.

The unfortunate consequence of protecting your kids is that, when circumstances eventually force your family to confront reality—whether it be a serious injury, a severe financial setback, or a life-threatening diagnosis—you (but most likely your kids) will be reacting in crisis mode. As a consequence, your options will most likely be dramatically restricted, and the pressure to make decisions quickly can become overwhelming.

We Don't Want to Face the Inevitable Transformation

The last part of your life can be a joyous time. You're freed from the constrictions and boundaries of the workaday world. You may be blessed with grandchildren, which offers another form of liberation (for example, "What happens at Grandma's, stays at Grandma's"). And you may have the opportunity to explore new corners of life that you could never find the time for in your younger years.

Because the good parts of this stage of life are so enjoyable, almost everyone I interviewed wanted to hold on to them for as long as possible by walling off the bad parts. The tool of choice was simple procrastination. You think: I'm not going to involve my kids in the issues surrounding my end of life until the time is right!

Of course, the time is never right—until it's too late. Often what happens is that the parent is suddenly stricken, mentally or physically—by dementia, a heart attack, or a fast-moving disease—and as a consequence, is unable to communicate coherently and effectively on the many decisions that need to be made.

Children could pay a huge, multidimensional emotional price for their parents' terminal procrastination:

- Guilt and feelings of inadequacy over the potentially adverse consequences of their decision making, especially when confronting conflicting opinions from various medical and legal professionals
- Shock over the difficulty of navigating the labyrinth of geriatric medicine
- Helplessness in dealing with the financial destruction created by the cost of geriatric care (In fact, one-third of all personal bankruptcies in America are a direct

result of healthcare expenses, especially those that occur in the last 18 months of life.)

- Long-term resentment among family members over the wisdom and consequences of decisions made on behalf of the parents in their last years of life

And this toll can linger for a lifetime.

We Want to Maintain Our Existing Parent-Child Relationship

For many of us, the most challenging and sensitive issues that we will come up against in the Other Talk concern the changes that we will experience in our senior years. I'm not referring to our evolving physical condition that we notice as we get older:

- Our stamina gets shorter.
- Our recovery time takes longer.
- Morning stiffness is part of waking up.
- Our row of plastic pill bottles gets longer.
- Looking for our reading glasses becomes an hourly event.
- Wondering why we just walked into a particular room becomes a regular occurrence.

All of this can be mildly annoying, but none of it is debilitating. The desire to maintain the status quo can be.

The Evolution of the Parent-Child Relationship

As I learned from the hundreds of interviews I conducted with families as well as doctors, nurses, and hospice workers, a fundamental and potentially difficult adjustment occurs as we age: the reversal of roles between parent and child that is triggered when you reach the point, physically and/or mentally, at which you can no longer operate independently.

In essence, the parent becomes the child, and the child becomes the parent.

Why is this reversal of roles so difficult and potentially life changing for both parties? Because it is not merely a mechanical reassignment of responsibilities. Rather, it shatters the relationship that you as a parent have had with your children since the day of their birth. As a result, you lose the power and control of being the adult, and your kids give up the security and freedom of being the children.

The Impact of Role Reversal on the Parents

For the parents, the hardest part of growing older may be the crushing realization that we're about to lose control of the life and lifestyle that we've worked so hard to create.

Despite all the successes you may have achieved throughout your life, all the good deeds you've bestowed on others, and all the love and support you've heaped on family and friends, at the end of life you may experience the fear of losing control.

As described by Kathleen, whom I interviewed for this book, it can start out as an uneasy premonition:

> Doing it our way isn't going to work indefinitely; in fact, I feel we're in this in-between stage, a time when we can still control how we live but not how much longer we're going to last or be able to make choices before we've become "too old."
>
> When I contemplate it, what we're really dealing with is, "How much longer can we continue to be us?"

I have learned, through my research, that the primary reason that the elderly begin to actively resist turning over responsibility and decision making to their offspring is their escalating fear of becoming powerless; becoming a burden on the family, physically and financially; losing their self-worth, self-respect, and dignity; and being abandoned by their family.

To make matters worse, since most people wait until a crisis hits before confronting the need to transfer power and control to the kids, role reversal is often forced on the parents with little or no discussion.

The Impact of Role Reversal on the Children

For the children, one of the hardest parts of seeing our parents age is the sinking feeling that we need to start taking responsibility for their lives physically, financially, and socially.

Typically for the kids, the shock of responsibility at the "moment of truth" is followed by feelings of inadequacy, embarrassment, and resentment as the plight of their parents comes to dominate their lives. This cauldron of emotional reactions is hardly surprising since the children who are about to take on the parent role often have little training and no warning that it's time to step into the caregiving role.

Unlike another major occurrence in life, childbirth, caregiving comes with no preparatory classes on issues and techniques; no predictable nine months of preparation; no showers to help with the expense of the responsibility; and no parent to turn to for advice or just a shoulder to cry on.

As a result, for the children with parental responsibility, the world of role reversal can be a very dark and lonely place. Again, the comparison with childbirth is instructive. With childcare, there are nine months to prepare; the evolution to term is usually predictable and straightforward; and there is generally a crowding around of family and friends to share in the event. With parent care, the catalyst is often a sudden, unexpected crisis; the decline is unpredictable and full of unpleasant surprises; and there is almost never any crowding around of family and friends to share in the event.

The bottom line is that the impact of the role-reversal process can be debilitating for both parent and child. Here's how Ralph, one of my research respondents, described the evolution:

> When we're kids, we don't think our parents know anything. When we grow up and have our own kids, we realize how smart our parents were.
>
> Then, when our parents are in a position either physically or mentally where they can't fend for themselves, we become their parent. They realize they've lost control.
>
> It's very scary; it's very hard; it's like a punch to the gut for them: "I'm not worth what I used to be."
>
> They go through all that; then you say, "Would you like to move to a nursing home?"

The Value of Stepping Up

I must admit that my first inclination in considering my responsibilities to my daughter was to perform another drive-by, similar to "the birds and the bees," sex books on the bed, and "any questions?" approach. Only this time it would be instructions on how to access the key to the safety deposit box, which contains a will, a life insurance policy, and a paid-up funeral service receipt.

Fortunately, having heard from my research respondents about the unintended consequences of the "goodbye drive-by," I realized that the Other Talk shouldn't just be about the necessary transactions at the end of life.

It should go beyond funeral and burial plans, wills, and donations to science. It needs to delve into the judgments and decisions that must be made and how your children will both have an impact on and be affected by them.

In essence, the Other Talk covers your life from here on. This will require some work on your part, both emotionally and rationally, but ultimately it will have powerful implications for your family's remaining time together.

The preparation begins with creating in yourself, then sharing with your kids, a tone and attitude that should permeate the Other Talk. You, the parent, are proactively taking the responsibility for empowering and preparing your kids for the reversal of roles that will take place in your later years. You, the parent, embrace the eventual reversal of roles not as giving up power and control but rather as achieving security and freedom.

The Other Talk will set the stage for a smooth transition when the time comes to shift decision-making responsibilities. Here's how: First, acknowledge the inevitability of the need for and the wisdom of transferring decision making and management of the day-to-day responsibilities. Second, discuss and establish ground rules on the potential circumstances or triggers that will effect the change of responsibilities for key functions such as bill paying, driving, living arrangements, money and asset management, and medical decisions.

Finally, the Other Talk culminates in a series of conversations that cover in depth how you would like to deal with four essentials:

1. Financing your uncertain future
2. Selecting the best living arrangements
3. Getting the medical care you need
4. Taking charge at the end of your life

Initially, the Other Talk may be uncomfortable for both you and your children, but as the first conversation unfolds and subsequent ones ensue, you and your family will begin to realize that you are empowering your kids for something that will have far-reaching and ongoing consequences for the rest of their lives.

In essence, the Other Talk can have a powerful impact on your children on a number of levels. It will help them cope with and successfully handle some of the difficult challenges that lie ahead for all of you. It will create a new dimension to the family relationship that comes from participating in, rather than suffering through, your last years. And it will teach them how to prepare for their own last years, giving your children a thorough understanding and actual experience for when they sit down with their own kids to have the Other Talk.

If you are still feeling hesitant or uneasy or unconvinced about having the Other Talk with your family, I would ask you to consider three questions that are addressed in the next three chapters:

1. What will happen if you don't have the Other Talk?
2. What can happen if you do have the Other Talk?
3. How can the Other Talk help you meet the unique challenges of your later years?

CHAPTER TWO

Recognizing the Negative Consequences of Silence

I didn't know what was going on in my body.
I just felt like a lot of weird things were going
on that I couldn't explain.

It was kind of like a free fall where you feel
like a kid who isn't understood, isn't heard.

I was confused, scared, didn't know where
to turn. So I decided just to wait it out.

—Richard, focus group participant

Whenever the hospice people would come
to visit, I'd turn off the television, wheel
Dad into the kitchen, and wait until they
left. I figured as long as they didn't come
through that door, we were safe.

—Kim, focus group participant

My great-grandfather, whom I called Grandpa, had a great life and a perfect ending.

Grandpa emigrated from Germany in his early thirties, and after working hard to learn English, he used his considerable woodworking skills to become a master carpenter. While he was often involved in building houses, he was best known for creating simple but elegant dining room tables and chairs.

When I got to know him, he was pushing 90 and living with his daughter and her husband (my grandparents), but he was still able to get around enough to tend to his rose garden.

One thing I really looked forward to was going over to watch the Chicago Cubs games with him. When they lost (which was often), he'd cuss them out with gusto (if Grandma wasn't around). Ahh, my first taste of male bonding at age eight!

One day in September we watched the Cubs win one and celebrated with a bowl of butter pecan ice cream (his favorite). Mom came to pick me up, and Grandpa headed outside to his rose garden and eventually dozed off. On this particular warm Indian summer afternoon, he didn't wake up.

Quick, painless, uncomplicated, in a place of his choosing, in a final moment of beauty and serenity.

No muss, no fuss, with a Cubs victory to send him on his way.

The Power of Procrastination and Inertia

Grandpa's demise came to be known in our family as the "rose garden exit strategy." Unfortunately, while this story was mildly amusing and, in some ways, comforting, over the years my parents began to firmly (wishfully?) embrace this fantasy of the end of life as their own.

As a result, this mindset allowed them to sweep all the challenges and unpleasantries of old age, and especially death, under the rug. If the subject ever came up with me or my two brothers, Mom and Dad's pat answer was always, "Everything will turn out just fine, so we don't need to talk about it."

What I learned when I began to research this book was that the vast majority of parents turn to that same stoic silence whenever confronted with issues or even questions about the last stage of life.

Through hundreds of conversations with families and eldercare and end-of-life practitioners, a pattern emerged as to how a parent's natural decline can unleash serious unwanted strains on the entire family relationship. My family's story demonstrates how the unintended consequences of stoic silence can play out.

Starting Down the Slippery Slope

When my parents reached their late sixties, they decided to sell their home healthcare business and finally retire to their house in the woods overlooking Lake Michigan. Then, to escape Michigan's harsh, gray winters, they transformed themselves into "snowbirds," buying a second home near Phoenix.

Life was great for the first couple of years of retirement. Many of Mom and Dad's friends from the Midwest had also decided to spend the winters in Phoenix, so there was a ready and comfortable group for them to tap into for trips into the desert and up the mountains, as well as cocktail hour at the end of the day. In addition, the recreation center down the street offered a pottery class and a garden club for Mom, and it had an outdoor swimming pool and woodworking shop for Dad.

My brothers and I and our wives and kids would go visit, typically in February, and everybody in the family felt that our parents' living arrangement seemed very workable. Dad had been diagnosed with multiple sclerosis (MS) 20 years earlier, but he was still getting around on a cane and was able to drive. Mom was as energetic and physically fit as she had always been, and she was able to effectively play the primary caregiver role. And since they had relocated to one of the retirement villages near Phoenix, there were plenty of medical and other support systems at their fingertips.

Then the crisis hit.

For me, it began on a Wednesday in late March. I was just finishing up a presentation of research findings to a group of senior executives in New York when an assistant came into the boardroom from a side door and handed me a note:

Your father's refusing to get into the ambulance. What do you want to do about it?

To say I was caught by surprise would be an understatement. I looked up at the assistant and indicated that I'd be right there. Once I reached the phone, the crisis began to take shape.

The paramedic said my father had taken a bad fall on the ceramic tile floor in their Spanish-influenced home and likely had fractured his hip but was refusing to go to the hospital. The paramedic described my mother's condition as frightened and incoherent, not surprising under the circumstances but also not her usual cool, calm, take-charge self.

Fortunately, my brother Doug had planned a trip out to Phoenix with his family and was, in fact, scheduled to arrive the next day. Unable to communicate with Mom, I got Dad on the phone and convinced him that the emergency room was the best place for him to be. Then I hung up the phone and called Doug to forewarn him that his trip out West was not going to be the usual visit.

Doug called me the next afternoon to describe a situation much worse than any of us had imagined. Dad had also fallen at least three other times in the preceding two weeks. Since Mom, at five-foot-three and 105 pounds, couldn't lift what was essentially dead weight, they called on their neighbor Bill to help get him back up, swearing him to secrecy from the family with "We don't want to worry them."

Then Doug discovered that the entire right side of my parents' Oldsmobile minivan was smashed in, the result of an accident Mom had had in a parking lot three weeks earlier.

Perhaps most depressing, my brother learned from our parents' doctor that Mom had been diagnosed with Alzheimer's, a horrendous disease that essentially peels away the brain one layer at a time while leaving the body intact. Dad apparently was going to tell us when they returned to Michigan the next summer.

I hung up the phone and felt a cold, numbing sensation of helplessness. As the afternoon turned into evening, the implications for me, my two brothers, and our families really began to sink in with a vengeance.

The Chilling Reality of Role Reversal

A parent care crisis is particularly devastating because reality hits you on two levels.

Reality number one for me and my two brothers was our total shock and anguish over our parents' deteriorated condition. Dad's MS had finally won the battle with his ability to walk so that he would be forever confined to a wheelchair. Equally disturbing, his disease had begun to aggressively attack his cognitive functions, particularly his short-term memory, organizational skills, and attention span. And Mom's Alzheimer's was rapidly stealing her ability to communicate. Within three months, she would never utter another coherent sentence.

While their crisis was sudden, their deterioration would be gradual. Mom would live another five years, although in a confused and increasingly frightened and antagonistic condition, and Dad would see another seven years, although in a world that swirled with conspiracies and hallucinations.

Reality number two was the sinking realization that Doug, Tom, and I, as well as our spouses, would be forced into the parental role with no planning, no expertise, inadequate resources, and most important, no direction from our parents.

We discovered that Dad had an investment portfolio that would cover the cost of a stable, healthy retirement scenario, but he had neglected to buy long-term-care insurance to pay for the expense of an extended physical decline of undetermined length. We were forced to quickly confront a series of complex and complicated decisions in the areas of financial planning and management, alternative living arrangements, medical care, and decision making at the very end of their lives.

To make this situation even more overwhelming, the three of us had never discussed any of these issues with our parents, and because of Dad's declining cognitive skills and Mom's increasing incoherence, we never would. As a result, we were, as the saying goes, sailing into uncharted waters without a compass.

Challenges Emerge

Clearly, Mom and Dad couldn't live on their own. But it was also obvious that we couldn't expect a logical, well-thought-out answer as to where they'd like to live, so we fell back on the only experience we'd had with a relative needing assisted living, which was Mom's mother.

At age 80, our grandmother decided to sell her two-story flat, where she had lived upstairs and rented out the lower floor. She was beginning to have trouble navigating the steps, and she had grown weary of dealing with renters, getting the house painted, and lining up plumbers, electricians, and yard maintenance.

So Grandma moved into an assisted-living senior center, where she had her own apartment, several dining rooms to choose from, a wide variety of social activities, and an extensive travel program that had her visiting someplace new every four months. In addition, there was an on-site advanced-care facility that she could turn to whenever her health required it.

At her ninetieth birthday party, she leaned over to me at dinner and confided, "I've just had the best 10 years of my life. You should try it!"

Using Grandma's experience as a model made the decision about what to do with Mom and Dad seem obvious: find a place that could replicate Grandma's experience (Doug offered to take that on in St. Louis, where he lived), and we would be finished.

The signs that this would be an unmitigated disaster began to crop up in the first month. Mom refused to leave their apartment except for meals with Dad, and Dad started getting increasingly aggressive and argumentative with the staff.

It only got worse a few months later when Dad (against doctor's orders) escaped to a college reunion in Ohio with the help of two fraternity brothers. Of course, he didn't tell anyone he was going, which after 24 hours resulted in panicky phone calls from the assisted-living facility as to his whereabouts and an escalating frenzy by my late-stage Alzheimer's mother, who was apparently feeling abandoned in a sea of strangers.

Desperate for a solution, I convened my two brothers and our wives to come up with a plan B, knowing that we couldn't expect any guidance from our parents in their current mental condition.

It finally dawned on us that our parents had always been a very sociable couple and that many of their friends from the garden club and their church still resided in their small town in Michigan. When we offered to move them back home, their beaming faces and excited body language told us that we were onto something.

But this path was also fraught with risk. We would need to create a reliable assisted-living support system—medically, physically, financially, and socially—in the middle of the woods, miles from their small downtown and nearly an hour from a hospital, with me in Chicago, Tom in D.C., and Doug in St. Louis.

The learning curve was steep, the time to execute was short, and along the way we hit many wrong turns and near disasters. Ultimately, keeping them in their home for the last part of their lives turned out to be the right thing. But that journey would have been so much easier, more direct, and less gut wrenching if we'd had a road map for where to go—and the time to chart how to get there.

Having the Other Talk would have provided us with just the tools we needed.

Battle Lines

The initial shock of reversing roles with our parents was only the beginning. Putting their full faith and confidence in a rose garden exit, Mom and Dad would cause a series of unexpected skirmishes between themselves and us that took a heavy emotional toll.

The Cadillac Moment

Dad had always been a self-sufficient, take-charge kind of guy; as a business owner, he had to be. But in his later years, when his bills started getting paid sporadically and he began running a hundred dollars in overdraft fees every month, I was forced to step in to take over the finances and what little nest egg was left. Not surprisingly, this set off a tug-of-war between the two of us that ran right up to his dying day.

But this battle for control wouldn't affect just me. I recall what my brothers and I call the "Cadillac moment," which crystallized how difficult the road ahead would be for all of us.

While Dad had apparently lost touch with the reality of money management, he was nothing if not stubborn and resourceful. I remember one weekend my wife, Pam, and I made the four-hour drive from Chicago to visit the folks. As I pulled into the driveway and opened the garage door, I saw my parents' van was gone. In its place sat a new Cadillac Eldorado.

When we got in the house, my first question was, "Dad, where's the van?"

"I traded it in for the Cadillac. I figured your mom and I deserved a little splurge," he replied with a sly, satisfied look on his face.

"But what did you use for money?" I asked incredulously.

"I cashed in the CDs at the bank."

As I sank into the old overstuffed couch in the living room, I realized that the loss of the $75,000 in CDs meant that my parents had finally reached insolvency. I sank deeper as it dawned on me that I would now need to inform my two brothers and our wives that we were on the hook for whatever expenses Medicare didn't cover. Worse yet, I couldn't tell them how long that financial obligation would last, but I could assure them that the debt was already considerable, due to the large home equity loan that Dad had taken out years ago to cover their overseas travels.

"Nothing Needs to Change"

My wife, Pam, remembers an equally telling anecdote about my mother:

When Tim and I got married, his mom welcomed me into the family like a long-lost daughter. What I really liked about her was the energy and passion that she brought not only to her family but also to her home.

Then, a couple of years ago, Mom started having accidents in the kitchen. Some of her favorite meals were turning out inedible when she mixed up ingredients. More and more of her prized antique glassware was getting broken. And when the fire department had to be called because she had left stove burners on to go watch TV, Tim and I knew it was time to move his parents to an assisted-living facility.

The movers had come in the day before to pack everything up. I kept Mom occupied with an extended shopping excursion and a long lunch at her favorite restaurant.

When I came downstairs the next morning, I found Mom surrounded by empty boxes marked "Kitchen stuff." All the contents had been put back in their accustomed places.

As I wended my way amid the boxes and piles of crumpled newspaper, she rose up to her full five feet, three inches, and fixed me with an icy stare I had never seen from her before.

"Pamela, dear," she said quietly but firmly, "Dad and I never agreed to move out of here, and that's not going to change. Now help me put this house back in order."

Casualties Along the Way

Our family made a number of mistakes along the way. But what really hurt was the disintegration of the loving, trusting relationship that had bound together the five of us and our extended families for so many years.

Here's how Tom, the youngest son, saw the crumbling family dynamic:

Mom was always the cheerleader, probably from her days as captain of the cheerleading squad at Northwestern football games. Her single-minded focus was on keeping the men in her life, her three sons and husband, even the dog, with a positive attitude, moving forward.

When Alzheimer's stripped her of her ability to speak and ultimately created an emotionless old woman, our family lost its catalyst.

The unfortunate consequence was to unleash Dad's paranoia and antagonism (which I later learned was inflamed by his MS) and cause confusion and resentments among all of us.

In my heart, I kept hoping she would get better, return as our spark plug, save us from the slow disintegration of our family.

Of course, she never did.

Here's how my brother Doug, the middle son, first experienced the breakdown of the family relationship when he showed up in Arizona the day after my forewarning phone call.

The moment he arrived at our parents' house, it became clear that their days of living independently in their home were long gone. Our father's mobility had deteriorated to the point that he was permanently relegated to a wheelchair. More ominous for both of them, our mother's Alzheimer's had rendered her dangerous in the kitchen and behind the wheel of her car. The depressing implication of their new reality was that our mother's role as caregiver and, therefore, guarantor of our parents' independent status, had come to an end:

I remember sitting with Mom in her kitchen, looking out at her prized grapefruit tree, trying to convince her that everything was going to be all right. As I struggled to come up with the words that would persuade her to give up that grapefruit tree and everything else that went with it so she and Dad could move into assisted living, I realized that we were asking her to stop being an adult.

We were telling her that she and my father were no longer capable of making intelligent decisions, of using good judgment, of managing their own money, of coming and going whenever they pleased, or of living in their own home.

We were telling her that, while she and Dad had done a great job of being an adult for the last 70 years, it was now time for them to be 6 years old again.

Her tears of anger and resentment are an image I'll never be able to shake.

As the oldest, my initial reaction was to focus on how to keep things together, wrestling with why and how and who would be responsible for the quality of life in my parents' last years. Yet ultimately, despite a considerable commitment of time and energy to this effort, my relationship with my proud, often stubborn father spiraled steadily downward.

Every time I was forced to take another step toward role reversal as my parents declined, I could sense from my father's angry words and body language that he saw it all as a conspiracy to steal his dignity. When I began to sell his stocks to pay for my parents' major medical bills and living expenses, he saw it as the destruction of his independence. When I took over the bill paying to put an end to the utility companies' threats to turn off the heat, lights, and phone, Dad detected a challenge to his manhood. And when I was forced to invoke a healthcare power of attorney to allow the ambulance driver to take my mother to the emergency room over my father's objections, he felt a personal affront to his authority.

Somehow I'd become the enemy, the one who was stealing things behind his back, the one who was constantly plotting to make his life miserable.

I wish we'd talked about this stuff when things were more normal!

Casualties Afterward

For many families who try to sweep end-of-life issues under the rug until it's too late, bad consequences don't end with the death of the parents. The story of Sara, Kate, and Jon, friends of mine since childhood, exemplifies the experience of many families I have spent time with in preparing to write this book.

My friends' parents hadn't done any real contingency planning for their last years, nor had they shared with their three children how they'd like decisions made when they were no longer physically and mentally capable of making those decisions themselves. As a result, the lives of Sara, Kate, and Jon were tragically altered in ways that their parents certainly didn't intend.

Jon, as the baby in the family, had grown up being taken care of by his two older sisters. So when the responsibilities of role reversal started piling up, he was at a loss as to what to do. Since his parents had created a vacuum for their kids by never having the Other Talk, Jon opted for the sidelines.

Ultimately, he took on the role of chief critic of his sisters' decision making, usually after the fact, and he rarely participated in the care of his parents. And when it became apparent that not only was there no estate left but there was a rather large debt that had been incurred for medical needs and assisted living, Jon blamed his sisters for this predicament and simply walked away from the family, even though he lived only 20 minutes away from his parents.

Kate, who became her parents' caregiver, suffered a fate that afflicts many adult children who attempt to deal with their parents' medical and emotional needs from a distance. Her employer, a large advertising agency in Chicago, valued her skill and accomplishments as an art director, and the company had cut her a good deal of slack to take care of her parents, who lived almost four hours away. But eventually her mounting caregiver responsibilities eroded her ability to perform in high-pressure situations that demanded a quick turnaround, and Kate lost her job.

Unfortunately, she has never found another job, which has put a severe strain on her family's finances and her relationship with her husband.

Sara, who took on the function of scheduling caregivers, paying bills, and generally keeping everything running on time, learned the hard way why 30 percent of bankruptcies in the United States are caused by overwhelming medical bills.

When her father's modest savings were depleted, Sara took out a home equity loan on her house to pay for her parents' expenses. When her father passed away, 18 months after her mother, Sara was faced with a bank loan that had reached 130 percent of the value of her house due to a real estate free fall; a formerly lucrative research business that had slowed to a crawl; a sister who had committed to help repay the home equity loan but now couldn't; and a brother who had abandoned the family.

Sara and her husband lost their house and begrudgingly tried to pick up the pieces after declaring bankruptcy. Ultimately, the situation proved too much for the two of them, ending in divorce.

It is safe to say that their parents didn't intend this outcome for their children.

It is also highly likely that if the two parents had embraced the concept of the Other Talk rather than desperately clinging to their version of the rose garden exit strategy, Sara, Kate, and Jon would be in a very different place today—emotionally, psychologically, and financially.

Silence That Can Engulf the Entire Family

I don't want to end this chapter by leaving the impression that silence on the aging process, consequences, and outcomes is embraced and, therefore, enforced only by the parents. In my research, I have come across many instances in which the entire family is complicit in building a wall around anything to do with the last stage of life.

Here's one example as told to me by Dr. Martha Twaddle, medical director of the Midwest Palliative & Hospice CareCenter:

According to the in-take sheet, the children are unaware of how sick their mother is.

On my initial visit, she was so weak, she couldn't lift her head up, her husband was feeding her, she was bed bound, and she couldn't get to the bathroom on her own. I said to myself, if she lives the next few days, it will be a miracle.

The kids are clueless, they have no idea, but they do know something's terribly wrong.

The kids won't go in her room. The husband won't cry. Even the dog's acting funny. Because everybody's trying to ignore it. They've been scared into an eerie silence.

CHAPTER THREE

Appreciating the Benefits of Family Collaboration

My first reaction when I heard about the rapid decline in my parents' physical state was this strange sense of panic. I'm a big-time corporate lawyer, for God's sake, and I don't panic for a living, but there I was. Mom and Dad refused to leave California, and my practice is in Michigan. Whom can I trust to be my eyes and ears out there? And what can I count on from my unemployed brother? And do I really expect to build a consensus, a coherent plan of action, with my drama-queen sister?

God, I wish we'd talked about this stuff when things were normal!

—Denise, focus group participant

In the hundreds of interviews I conducted, I heard a number of tales that mirrored my own experiences as well as those of Jon, Kate, and Sara. While each narrative contained its own unique mix of details, most of my storytellers ended with the same conclusion: "I'll never put my kids through what just happened to me!"

Yet they most likely will, just as the generations before them did, because the prospect of talking about dying and role reversal has a way of freezing even the most resolute person.

I might have followed in their footsteps except for two catalysts that jump-started my wife, Pam, and me into action. The first was the Terri Schiavo saga; the second was a nearly "lights-out" experience on a sailboat.

The Destruction of a Family

In February 1990, a woman named Terri Schiavo suddenly collapsed while at home, and oxygen was cut off from her brain for several minutes. The result was severe brain damage. Although she could breathe and maintain a heartbeat on her own, she needed a feeding tube connected to her stomach to keep her alive.

The story of her next 15 years had a painful, ultimately destructive impact on her family, but it also created profound ethical, philosophical, and emotional implications for the entire country, including my wife and me. In fact, it was the springboard that set us on a journey that would culminate in our developing the concept of the Other Talk.

While the Terri Schiavo case eventually spiraled into a battle royal between right-to-die and right-to-life partisans, each egged on by self-serving politicians, the crux of the matter boiled down to the question, What did Terri want done at the end of her life?

According to her husband, Michael Schiavo, Terri would not have wanted to be kept alive by artificial means. He claimed she had told him, "If I ever have to be a burden to anybody, I don't want to live like that."

"My aim is to carry out Terri's wishes," Michael told a reporter two years into the protracted court proceedings. "If Terri ever knew that I had somebody taking care of her bodily functions, she'd kill us all in a heartbeat. She'd be so angry!"

Terri's parents, Bob and Mary Schindler, passionately called into question Michael's assertions. They maintained that it would be totally out of character for Terri to take such a stance because she was a devout Roman Catholic who believed in the sanctity of life.

Unfortunately, there was nothing in writing to back up either side's position. Worse yet, Terri was ultimately reduced to a pawn that was fought over by the two warring factions. Her feeding tube was disconnected for three days in April 2001 before a court reversed the order, and again for six days in January 2003, until another legal challenge put it back in.

On March 18, 2005, her feeding tube was removed one more time. She died at a hospice facility in central Florida on March 31.

While none of us will ever know what Terri wanted done at the end of her life, it's safe to say that her on-again, off-again existence, with its corollary of a highly toxic family dynamic, is not what she or anyone else would wish for.

A Catalyst for the Other Talk

Terri's plight and the tearing apart of her family affected millions of people from around the world in a variety of ways. And it led Pam and me to sit down with our 34-year-old daughter, Dakota, a Montessori teacher, and her 36-year-old husband, Fernando, a manager of Internet operations, to talk about the implications of the Schiavo case for our family.

Initially, the conversation revolved around the chaos and heartbreak that were generated by the tug-of-war between Terri's husband and her parents. But it would evolve into a deeper discussion of what we as a group could do to avoid the train wreck that had engulfed Terri and her family.

As I discovered in researching the Schiavo case, two legal documents serve that exact purpose. Taken together, the *durable power of attorney for healthcare* and the *healthcare proxy* allow individuals to appoint someone to make healthcare decisions on their behalf if they are incapacitated by a debilitating illness or a serious injury. The four of us agreed that these would be important documents to have—for Pam and me, if one of us were suddenly stricken as Terri was, and for Dakota and Fernando, if Pam and I reach the point that we are unable physically or mentally to deal with healthcare decisions.

Then the discussion turned to the key issue of the Schiavo case: What did Terri want done at the end of her life? Because there were no written instructions from her, Terri's parents and husband spent years fighting over diametrically opposed interpretations of what Terri might have wanted.

As I dug deeper into the advance-directive world, I discovered that there exists a legal document called a *living will* that provides instructions on the course of treatment that healthcare providers, caregivers, and healthcare proxy designees must follow in the event that an individual is unable to make and communicate healthcare decisions.

Ever the teacher, Dakota suggested that, as a learning exercise, we each think about, and then write down, how Pam and I might compose our own personal living wills.

The next week, as the four of us began to share our opinions on the content of the two living wills, we were surprised to discover a variety of interpretations of what Pam or I would want to happen.

Fernando assumed that I would want to fight until my last dying breath and that Pam would want things ended if she were put on a feeding tube for more than a week. Dakota followed the route of keeping us both going by artificial means, in case a cure was somehow discovered. Pam and I both guessed wrong on the other's wishes, primarily because we had never had nor wanted to have this conversation. We all agreed that we would meet again after Pam and I returned from an upcoming vacation to Italy, to work out more precise interpretations and legal descriptions of our wishes at the end of our lives.

Little did I know that I was headed for an up-close-and-personal interaction with the price of leisurely postponement and procrastination.

My Call to Action

The trip was an eight-day bike tour through the lush and hilly countryside of Tuscany. At the end of the cycling excursion, Pam and I headed off for some R&R in Cinque Terre, a collection of wonderfully picturesque villages perched on hills overlooking the Mediterranean Sea. No cars were allowed, so the only way to travel was on foot, or by ferry or train. Or to commission a 45-foot sailboat, which sounded like great fun, and it would certainly be safe enough since the vessel came with a skipper and a crew. We chose the sailboat.

The boat was indeed spectacular. The captain and his mates had spent almost a year restoring and refinishing the teak mast, flooring, and a boom that was almost 20 feet long. (More about that boom in a moment.)

When we left the dock, the skipper kept the sails furled and instead used the motor to get from town to town, giving us a running commentary about the beautifully quaint homes that clung to the sides of the cliffs overlooking the sea.

After an hour of this, I started pestering the crew to put up the sails, turn off the engine, and head out into the Mediterranean. They eventually acquiesced.

Twenty minutes into the sail, a sudden strong wind came up, and it quickly dawned on me from the looks of panic on their faces that the crew members were boat refinishers, not boat navigators.

As the only experienced sailor on the boat, I told the skipper to head into the wind and hold it there while I worked with the crew to bring down the sails. Two minutes later, the skipper decided to help with the sails, leaving the tiller unattended, which caused the boat and that 20-foot teak boom to begin to rock violently from side to side. That's the last image I remember of being on the boat.

My next recollection is of lying on a gurney in a chaotic and fairly rudimentary emergency room. I couldn't move. I couldn't speak. I couldn't even make a sound. But I could think, and what began to roll through my mind was the conversation about end-of-life decisions that Pam and I and the kids had left unfinished until after the bike trip. Would our procrastination mean that we would suffer the same fate as the Schiavo family?

Fortunately I recovered, although it took 50 stitches across the top of my skull, where that teak boom had landed. Needless to say, in light of my brush with potential paralysis, brain damage, or worse, the family quickly put into writing the directions and thought processes that Pam and I wanted followed when and if it came time to invoke our respective healthcare documents.

How the Other Talk Evolved

An important epiphany grew out of my encounter with that 20-foot-long teak boom. In addition to establishing written contingency plans in the form of living wills, healthcare powers of attorney, and proxy designations, Pam and I executed wills, took out life insurance policies, and developed a retirement income and spending plan.

Many people would say that these actions constitute the full extent of long-term planning for this stage of life. But it dawned on us that we could do better. We had come to realize that, while we were still physically, mentally, and emotionally sharp, we needed to be talking with our kids not just about what to do at the end medically but also about the challenges, difficult decisions, changing roles, and shifting responsibilities that Dakota and Fernando will undoubtedly be part of between now and then.

We realized that we needed to include in the Other Talk a discussion of decisions to be made at the end as well as the issues of life that span the entire last years of life, including financing our uncertain future, selecting the best living arrangements, getting the medical care we need, and taking charge at the end of life.

Finally, it struck us that our plan should also include trigger points for when a particular responsibility needs to shift from parent to child. This is especially important because the deterioration of cognitive and physical abilities is often gradual and not as noticeable (or admissible) to the parent as it is to the kids. That's why planning for it has to be done early.

As a result, we developed criteria that we all four could agree to but that would ultimately empower Dakota and Fernando to make the decision on, say, when, if, and how to change our living arrangements. It would be much better for them, and ultimately for us, if we discussed those decisions early.

The Two-Way Benefits

By sitting down with Dakota and Fernando to have the Other Talk, Pam and I were preparing ourselves and our family for what was to come while also establishing an environment in which we could focus much more on all the living that is ahead of us.

In addition, not only has our family thoroughly aired the potential decision points that could emerge in Pam's and my last years, but we have also committed for the past three years to review and update it annually. This "annual checkup" approach benefits both the parents and the kids.

How? For Pam and me, it encourages us explicitly to recognize that our physical and financial condition will likely change in unexpected ways and that our assumptions and beliefs may shift over time. For Dakota and Fernando, as their own personal, job, and family responsibilities evolve, the annual checkup allows them to reevaluate and discuss the roles they are able to play in our last years.

On a more personal level, everybody in the family had his or her own take on how the Other Talk is making an impact on our lives together:

PAM: What I like about this approach is that it clarifies for me that parenting doesn't end with our kids' surviving high school or graduating from college or getting married or becoming parents. It ends with preparing for and participating with our children in their role in our last years. In fact, I believe that Tim and I will be making things a little bit easier for Dakota and Fernando as we get older. And hopefully we will show them how to do that for their kids as well.

DAKOTA: Dealing with my parents' future before there are panicky late-night phone calls or surprising overdue bills is a gift. I feel prepared, and so do they. Questions I didn't even know I would have to answer have already been thought through by the people most affected by them.

What the talk taught me, busy with a toddler and not thinking about retirement, was not only how important it is to prepare for my parents' end of life but also how to model the talk I will have with my son one day.

FERNANDO: While the point of the Other Talk was for Pam and Tim to share with us how they wanted to approach their last years, it also gave Dakota and me a chance to reflect on how their choices might impact us. In addition, it helped prepare us for becoming Dakota's parents' "parents" without the typical drama and bad feelings that I've seen in other families. Finally, it got me thinking about how to broach the subject of the Other Talk with my own parents.

CHAPTER FOUR

Navigating the Baby Boomers' Perfect Storm

The baby boom generation has always felt secure, knowing that our last chapter will be longer, wealthier, healthier than our parents'. Imagine our surprise when we arrive to find the eldercare infrastructure overwhelmed and crumbling.

—Carlos, physician and
focus group participant

If you've read this far, I'm hoping you are now intrigued by what the Other Talk can offer you and your family: a chance to discuss with your kids the various issues and options that arise in the last years of life; an opportunity to create a road map for decision making during the inevitable role reversal that will occur as you get older; and an occasion for you to teach, probe, think about, and share ideas with your kids about the end of life—not only dying but also coping with the aging process.

And if you are in this generation, the Other Talk you have will be uniquely your own because you will experience your last years in ways previous generations never did, as you have with every other stage of life.

The good news is, of course, that you will be able to enjoy a longer, healthier, more active lifestyle in your senior years. And with the unprecedented wealth accumulation piled up by this generation, according to Fidelity Investments, you can expect to have a whole lot more fun.

The flip side of these happy circumstances is what makes the Other Talk not just an opportunity for you to bond with your kids but also an imperative if you are to have any hope of managing the rest of your life. The reason, quite simply, is that a "perfect storm" has been brewing in geriatric care in recent years, and it will wreak increasing havoc as more and more of us reach 65. This means that you and your family are going to need a real sense of urgency to plan and prepare for a whole new set of challenges when you enter your last years.

Here are the three phenomena that power this generation's perfect storm: an escalating demand for resource-intensive healthcare, greater longevity, and a declining supply of medical practitioners.

An Escalating Demand for Resource-Intensive Healthcare

Starting in 2010, the 77 million baby boomers began our march into retirement. This unprecedented demographic movement will continue to have a profound impact on U.S. society and its healthcare system for generations to come.

In 2011 alone, the number of people in the United States celebrating their sixty-fifth birthday jumped 21 percent, from 2.7 million to 3.3 million, according to 2010 U.S. Census Bureau projections.

The ranks of Americans aged 65 and older are projected to more than double by 2050, from 40.2 million to 88.5 million. They'll comprise 19 percent of the population in 2030, compared to 13 percent in 2013. The 85-and-older population will be our fastest-growing segment, projected to grow from 5.8 million to 19 million by 2050, according to the U.S. Administration on Aging.

The implications of this tidal wave of new geriatric patients are momentous in part because of the sheer numbers alone but also because of the type of healthcare involved: the average retiree requires healthcare that is many times more resource intensive than the average American. In fact, the 13 percent of our population over 65 today uses a disproportionate amount of services, according to a 2009 study by the American Hospital Association:

- 44 percent of hospital care
- 38 percent of emergency medical service responses
- 35 percent of prescriptions
- 26 percent of physician visits

Finally, it's worth noting that in general, the number of family caregivers is dwindling, for several reasons. First, Americans are having smaller families than generations have had in the past. Second, Americans' greater geographical mobility means your kids may be dispersed across the country and less available for caregiving. And third, dual-career households mean that the traditional stay-at-home wife taking care of Mom and Dad is often no longer an option.

While the ramifications of the baby boomer takeover of the retirement segment may be multilayered, complicated, and daunting for the healthcare community, they are quite simple for you and your family as you enter your final years: from now on, the competition for geriatric healthcare resources will become fiercer with each passing year.

You and your kids need to start preparing.

Greater Longevity

The duration of the "elderly" years has mushroomed over the past three decades, as life expectancies have increased for older Americans. In fact, an American who reaches age

65 can expect to live on average another 18.5 years (16.8 for men, 19.8 for women), according to the National Center for Health Statistics.

But there is a downside to all those extra years. The fundamental drivers of this increasing longevity are the groundbreaking medical advancements that have been made in the detection, diagnosis, and treatment of health issues, along with a more concerted commitment to healthy living. The result is that people are dying gradually rather than suddenly, which was the norm in previous generations. For example, according to an annual study by the Centers for Disease Control and Prevention, deaths from heart attacks have dropped 61 percent from the rates of 30 years ago. Stroke fatalities have declined even further, 71 percent, over this same period.

Of course, people are still dying; they're just taking longer to do it. In recent years, "incremental killers" have become much more common. Deaths from chronic respiratory disease have increased 77 percent in the last 15 years. Deaths from Alzheimer's disease increased 68 percent between 2000 and 2010, and the number of global cancer deaths is projected to increase 45 percent from 2007 to 2030.

The upshot is that the cost implications of living longer lives are significant. As older Americans make up a larger proportion of the population, the resulting increase in the numbers of people with chronic health conditions like Parkinson's disease, arthritis, diabetes, heart disease, and almost all types of cancer will create a huge demand for healthcare and social services.

To add to the strain on an already challenged medical care delivery system, as of 2014, approximately 30 million more Americans than in the past will have access to health insurance under the Affordable Care Act.

The implication for you and your family is that longer life will very likely mean a greater need for the family to cover assisted-living and medical expenses.

You and your kids need to start preparing.

A Declining Supply of Medical Practitioners

What ultimately whips the world of geriatric care into a perfect storm is that the exploding demand is about to run into faltering supply.

Over the next 30 years, our sheer numbers and the extent and duration of our medical requirements will drive up the need for quality healthcare exponentially. Yet practitioners who deliver geriatric medical care—primary care physicians, nurse practitioners, and geriatricians—are already in short supply, and their numbers are projected to fall further behind exploding demand, as can be seen in this illustration.

The Declining Supply of Medical Practitioners

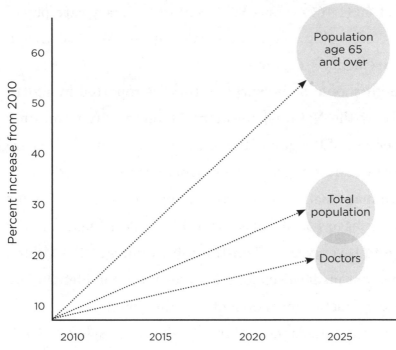

Sources: U.S. Census Bureau and Association of American Medical Colleges

Primary Care Physicians

Primary care physicians are critical to the care management of the chronic conditions that older Americans will inevitably face. Yet, just as we baby boomers are entering this phase of our lives, medical students have been opting for the specialties.

In 1960, half of all physicians in the United States were in primary care. By 1978, the percentage had fallen to 36 percent, and in 2010, it was down to 33 percent. The root causes for this migration appear to be a combination of lifestyle and compensation. Specialists generally have shorter hours and limited on-call schedules. Yet their median income sits at $384,467, versus $212,840 for primary care physicians, according to a 2012 survey by the Medical Group Management Association.

So it should be no surprise that, as reported in a 2013 study by the National Resident Matching Program, only 39 percent of the graduating classes of medical schools are entering residency training in primary care.

To make matters worse, the number of federally funded residencies has been frozen since 1997. (Residencies are the three to seven years of on-the-job training in the United States that medical school graduates must complete before they can practice independently in this country.)

Medicare funds most of the residencies, paying $9.5 billion a year to subsidize 94,000 positions at teaching hospitals. Medicaid and other sources fund about 10,000 more. But as baby boomers and new beneficiaries of the Affordable Care Act flood the market and demand accelerates, government support for residencies (future doctors) remains static.

But there's also a qualitative challenge that this generation will need to confront, as described by an internist in one of my focus groups:

Because fees are fixed by Medicare and insurers, the only way primary care doctors can generate more revenue is to take on more patients, which means spending less time with each one. Yet the most common complaint you hear from patients is, "I don't have enough time with the doctor."

They're right. You can't take good care of your patients with chronic conditions in less than 15 minutes.

Nurses

The picture is equally dire in the nursing profession. Today, more than 8 percent of nursing positions nationwide are vacant.

To make matters worse, dramatic technological improvements in healthcare in the last 20 years mean even more nurses are required, especially those with comprehensive training, because there are more diagnostic tests to run, more medications to administer, and more machines to monitor. Demand for registered nurses is expected to grow 26 percent from 2010 to 2020, according to government statistics.

Geriatric Specialists

Then there are the geriatricians—that is, doctors who have taken an additional year of training after a three-year residency in family or internal medicine. In many ways, this practitioner group is uniquely qualified to treat older Americans because, rather than just focusing on cures, they also spend time helping patients to maintain their independence and to age as well as possible.

Yet perhaps because geriatricians average $240,000 a year in salary, about half of what radiologists, gastroenterologists, and cardiologists make (according to the American Medical Group Association), their numbers have fallen by one-third in recent years. In fact, today there are only 7,600 geriatricians nationwide—not enough to meet current demand and far below the 36,000 needed by 2030, according to the American Geriatrics Society.

Home Care and Nursing Home Aides

Finally, there is a growing shortage of support staff in this field. Just as my generation heads into retirement, reports an April 2013 *Wall Street Journal* article, "nursing homes and operators providing home-care services already are straining to find enough . . . care workers." This is a particularly acute problem because most of the demand in geriatric care is for one-on-one custodial care. These workers help with things like bathing, grooming, dressing, meal preparation, transportation, social services, and shopping—help that can't be automated as the demand for these services escalates.

The clear implications for you and your family are that the days of your doctor providing continuity of care and guiding you through the complex medical system are most likely numbered, leaving you to navigate on your own.

Available Public Resources

Starting in 2010, an enormous segment—43 percent—of the working population began to retire and transform from taxpayers to government beneficiaries, according to the Census Bureau. Because the next generation is 34 percent smaller than my generation, the workforce will grow more slowly, as will tax revenues to finance Medicare, Medicaid, and Social Security. At the same time, healthcare inflation, which is driving up the bill for Medicare and Medicaid, could send the federal budget deficit skyrocketing.

While we won't know the outcome of the current debate about medical spending priorities and budget deficits raging in Congress and across the country, perhaps for years to come, it's obvious that changes to the delivery of medical care to older Americans will occur.

One thing we do know for certain: the rules of the game and public resources available will look vastly different than they do today.

Clearly, you and your kids need to start preparing.

You should have the Other Talk now—then keep on talking!

You need a game changer if you are to successfully navigate the medical and many other challenges that you will face in your later years.

The Other Talk is one important tool to help you achieve that because you need partners (your kids) and a plan that prepares you and your family for the roles you all will play in your later years.

And because you can't know how things will turn out, you'll need to have the Other Talk on an ongoing basis. The next two parts of the book will show you how.

PART TWO

Getting Ready for the Other Talk

As our parent care crisis mushroomed, my brothers and I became so busy solving problems—

- Arranging and rearranging living conditions
- Negotiating with doctors and insurance companies and Medicare administrators
- Determining the extent of the financial assets
- Dispensing with the stack of unpaid bills
- Selling cars and furniture and a garage full of stuff

—that we lost sight of the most important need: facing this most human of experiences together.

—Jason, focus group participant

CHAPTER FIVE

Setting the Stage

It was quite unnerving to see how quickly the winds of our parent care crisis morphed into a full-blown tornado, sucking in family members and family resources with relative ease.

—Thomas, focus group participant

Current conventional wisdom has it that our generation will age differently than our parents'. We will have a more active lifestyle, more dollars to spend on it, and more years to enjoy it.

But there is one aspect of aging in which we will surely follow in the footsteps of all previous generations. Like every elderly parent in the history of humankind, we will undoubtedly intone with somber and heartfelt conviction, "I don't want to be a burden to my kids."

Well, get over it. You probably will be! Because as we cruise through our last years of life, we will need help—and plenty of it.

Margaret, a social worker I interviewed from the south side of Chicago, gave me a sense of reality by laying out the breadth and depth of what's involved:

> It's a full-time job when you are looking out for elderly people who have long-term care needs that are chronic and who have declining health . . . from the handling of their day-to-day care, to running the gauntlet of insurance, Medicare, and Medicaid forms and regulations, to learning about various diseases and the myriad of alternative (and often conflicting) treatments, to the managing of medications and doctor visits.
>
> It's a full-time job! And all this at a time when the adult child is scrambling to keep the many balls in his or her own life (like kids, spouse, household, career) from crashing to the ground.

Of course, the way to reduce the weight of this burdensome responsibility is to start *now* to have the Other Talk. By brainstorming and fleshing out the contingencies, preparing for the surprises, and making your last years of life a time for your family to enjoy together, not just a trauma to stumble through, you will be lightening the load considerably.

Yet there seems to be a catch-22 in play whenever this conversation is contemplated.

On the one hand, I have found that the basic concept and construct of the Other Talk meets with nearly universal enthusiasm, whether I'm talking with colleagues in the elder-care, hospice, and funeral service industries, with professionals in the publishing and academic worlds, or with members of my generation or even with their gen X kids. They get it: the wisdom of involving your kids in the issues and decisions that come up during your last years; the tremendous emotional benefits of avoiding family feuds, financial surprises, and philosophical disagreements; and the ability to focus on the living to be done rather than the dying to be feared.

On the other hand, I also know from my research with families that the theory of the Other Talk rarely translates into practice. It's as if a locked door stands between the parents and the kids. One or maybe both parties may actually want to engage in the conversation. But what causes them to hold back are the very difficult emotional issues and various fears of the unknown that can bubble up around the end of life.

That's why it's critical that you do a good deal of emotional and strategic preparation before you are ready to open the door to the Other Talk.

There are four steps to setting this stage effectively:

1. Start with your own mental state.
2. Factor in the kids' emotions.
3. Establish a frame of reference.
4. Adopt a comfortable tone.

Step 1. Start with Your Own Mental State

Just as they did when you sat them down for that first "birds and the bees" talk, your kids will take cues and clues from you on how open and comfortable you are in discussing your last years, which will influence how willing they are to participate in the conversation.

As a result, before you can initiate the Other Talk, you'll need to confront and ultimately come to grips with two practical yet emotion-laden issues: role reversals and your finances.

Role Reversals

Many of us define ourselves by our accomplishments, our skills at getting things done, and our abilities to develop creative solutions to complex problems. These barometers of success translate into power and control over our lives and ultimately our sense of self-worth.

Therefore, when we agree to the reversal of roles with our kids, however willingly, we may tend to feel that turning over power and control for decision making will diminish our self-image. As a consequence, even for the parent who acknowledges the need and inevitability of role reversal, it can still carry the stigma of, "I am no longer who I was!"

A good example of this internal conflict is Dan, a successful entrepreneur in Seattle, who recently signed over financial and medical powers of attorney to his eldest son. In addition, Dan, along with his wife, Shari, moved out of their three-story house into a well-appointed assisted-living facility. He had done all of this voluntarily after several conversations with his doctor, financial advisors, and extended family, but clearly he felt a deep sense of loss:

> I know Shari and I need assistance at this point in our lives, but, damn it, I feel like I had to give up a huge part of me.
>
> I've always been proud of my accomplishments, growing the company from 2 to 200 people, attracting great young talent, positioning the firm as a player on the national stage. And I really enjoyed my success in the stock market.
>
> Now my affairs are managed by my kids—and I deeply appreciate the time and energy that they put into it. But there are times when I want to stand up and scream, "You can't tell me what to do. I changed your diapers!"

Clearly, the notion of role reversal can stir up some serious emotional reactions. That's why the Other Talk puts it front and center in the conversation. The intended consequence is that when the time comes to shift decision-making responsibilities, it is accomplished more like the smooth transition of a pendulum, rather than an abrupt hitting the wall at the moment of crisis. To ensure a comfortable pendulum swing, you should reconcile yourself to role reversal on three levels.

First, openly acknowledge the inevitability of ceding the decision making and managing of the day-to-day responsibilities to your kids. This will focus you on planning to hand off these responsibilities, rather than grappling to hang on to them.

Second, establish ground rules on the potential circumstances or trigger points that will affect the change of responsibilities in key functions, such as bill paying, transportation, living arrangements, money and asset management, and medical decisions.

Finally, embrace your plan for role reversal as liberating, not denigrating. It's not the loss of power and control; it's the gain of security and freedom. It's not about where the pendulum is swinging from; it's where the pendulum is headed.

Full Financial Disclosures

The other hurdle that you need to get over is when and how much of your financial situation you are willing to share with your kids. (The irony, of course, is that your financial reality, good or bad, will end up on your kids' plate anyway.) The short answer if you are serious about having the Other Talk is, "Now, and everything."

This is apparently easier said than done. When I asked my research respondents whether they had shared their financial reality with their kids, they came up with a variety of excuses for why they hadn't:

"It's none of their business." (My response: "It will be.")

"I'm embarrassed that I didn't save enough for retirement."
(My response: "That's a really excellent reason why they should know!")

"My kids aren't capable of managing financial details."
(My response: "Your family definitely needs a plan and maybe some outside help.")

"Telling my kids how large the estate is could have unintended consequences on their lifestyle and motivations." (My response: "Discussing family finances now will be much better than waiting until after the sibling battle lines form.")

To a large extent, the Other Talk is about contingency planning. Without having a thorough discussion with your kids now about your financial situation, you're essentially tying one hand behind their backs just as they are getting ready to take on more responsibilities in your last years.

You need to prepare yourself to work with your kids *now* to understand what's available financially, introduce them to any financial advisors you might have, and educate them on your asset allocation and spending strategies. That's the partnership that the Other Talk is designed to achieve between you and your kids.

Step 2. Factor in the Kids' Emotions

Once you've gotten your own head straight with the emotional hurdles of role reversals and financial disclosures, it's time to consider the kids' mindset on the eve of the Other Talk. As you get ready to unlock that door, swing it open, and invite the kids in for your first Other Talk conversation, it's important that you think about how to prepare them mentally and emotionally for the subject matter.

To begin with, you need to recognize that every question or issue related to the end of your life, however mundane, is a mix of practical and emotional dimensions. In fact, you can expect a jumble of reactions that can be wide-ranging and, at times, contradictory: fear, sadness, nervousness, anger, queasiness, panic, and revulsion, to name a few.

Why this bewildering array of seemingly disparate reactions? Because you're talking about coping with a period of undetermined time that may include several stages, but with an ending where your kids are left without a parent.

There's also another emotional dimension to the Other Talk. Kids can become overwhelmed with feelings of responsibility, guilt, inadequacy, embarrassment, and resentment as the fear and foreboding of what is to come next pulls into view.

For both emotional traumas, loss of a parent and the burden of caregiving, it's critical that you carefully prepare your kids for the Other Talk. You'll need to think about which issues are troubling or even terrifying, and to which child. You'll need to help the family get past the fear of confronting your mortality; of brushing up against the issues of power, control, and financial limitations; of visualizing what it will be like when you are gone.

My first suggestion to get your kids ready emotionally is only slightly self-serving, since it has been reported to be very effective by a number of families who have reviewed this book: give your kids a copy to read *before* you sit down for the Other Talk.

This technique seems to help pave the way because your kids are able to explore and embrace the philosophy of pro-actively dealing with possible events in your last years before they happen. It allows the kids to deal with the hypothetical events before confronting their eventual reality.

My second suggestion is that you discuss with your spouse how your individual attitudes, desires, and opinions may differ, sometimes markedly, and how they should be woven into the conversation in a way that doesn't cause confusion or conflict. What you don't want to do is confront all these issues for the first time in front of the kids.

My third suggestion is to encourage your kids to adapt the collaborative theme inherent in the Other Talk in terms of how they might work with their brothers and sisters during your last years. We know definitively that the impact of being saddled, often unexpectedly, with the burden of parental care can have serious repercussions among siblings.

In a National Alliance for Caregiving and AARP study, 17 percent of those surveyed said the responsibility of caring for their loved ones had taken a toll on their health, while 31 percent described the situation as emotionally stressful. Two-thirds of those caregivers who had jobs said they had gone to work late, left early, or taken time off because of their caregiving responsibilities.

It doesn't have to be this way. Recently I witnessed how the Other Talk can help create a sense of purpose and cooperation with a family I spoke with in Phoenix. The son, Robert, assumed responsibility for his mother's finances. Daughter Vanessa handled the medical appointments. The youngest child, Christy, acted as the day-to-day contact for the home healthcare nurses.

Creating a care arrangement as the family in Phoenix did can not only achieve collaboration of effort and commitment but can also prevent one person's being overwhelmed as the primary caregiver, which typically is a daughter or the oldest child who lives closest to the parents.

Step 3. Establish a Frame of Reference

The next step in your preparation is to frame the conversation and the participants' role in it so that you can achieve good outcomes and avoid panic and stress; manage your affairs the way you intend; avoid choices you don't want;

and ensure that everyone contributes in ways that match their interests, skill sets, and comfort level.

Additionally, it's important to establish that the Other Talk is not a onetime event, à la "the birds and the bees" drive-by, with books on the bed and, "Any questions?" Rather, it is an ongoing, dynamic dialogue because your physical and financial conditions will likely change in unexpected ways, your assumptions and beliefs may evolve over time, and the availability of your kids may change due to shifting job and family responsibilities, resources, and geographic location.

Finally, because you want to be proactive in managing your last years, not just reactive to tomorrow's surprises or emergencies, you and your kids should plan to commit time and energy to two fundamental functions: the knowledge base and trigger points.

Our Knowledge Base

As I mentioned in Chapter 4, the dynamics of geriatric care are going to change dramatically in the years ahead as a result of an escalating demand for resource-intensive healthcare, elderly and chronic care patients who will be living longer than in previous generations, the declining supply of geriatric practitioners, and the questionable availability of public resources for people who are elderly and disabled.

As a result, the rules of the game are changing, and to a large extent, you and your family will be on your own to figure out options and answers. You will need to learn a lot, be organized, and keep up with current trends. That's why staying on top of your options, emerging medical treatments, and changing legal and financial regulations will become a critical ongoing function for the entire family.

I believe that the Other Talk is the place to start parceling out research assignments, and in subsequent Other Talks, it is the place where you all can come together to review, update, and cross-reference your knowledge base.

To give you a sense of how extensive this imperative will most likely be for you, let me introduce Carly, a 45-year-old accountant and daughter of a Parkinson's patient:

> I have a binder that's about four inches thick, with all the things that I had to find out about in all these different areas, from insurance forms, rules, and regulations to new medical treatments, new sources of funding, and new living arrangements to speech therapists, occupational therapists, and physical therapists to Medicare, Dad's pension, and Social Security.
>
> It's relentless, it's overwhelming . . . and absolutely essential.

Trigger Points

Perhaps one of the most challenging issues that your family will face in your last years is how and when to shift decision making from you to your kids. That's why a key dimension of the Other Talk is to establish criteria that will trigger the decisions to reassign roles and responsibilities.

The intent of all this is to avoid your feeling threatened and confrontational when the time comes to make a change because you've already agreed to it up front.

To begin with, it is important to recognize that role reversal doesn't need to be a onetime wholesale changing of the guard. Rather, it can be a series of trigger points for the various functions of day-to-day living (paying the bills, moving out of your house, etc.).

The essence of establishing trigger points is that you and your kids thoroughly discuss and jointly decide how and when a particular responsibility is to be shifted. In this way, your entire family feels a part of the decision and can take ownership in its implementation.

While I'll be discussing the trigger-point concept in later chapters, let me demonstrate how it can work with what is often the opening act in a family's role reversal: giving up the car keys.

For your kids, the decision for you to stop driving has important practical implications. It means that your loss of mobility will require your children and you to come up with alternate forms of transportation: their chauffeuring you, if they live in town, or your depending on friends and neighbors, taxis, and public transportation.

For you, this change of life is more cerebral, more fundamental. Here's my personal take on it:

- I love driving, especially in my blue sports car,
  a Nissan 350Z.
- I love the freedom of getting up and going whenever
  I want.
- I love the sensation of smoothly shifting through
  six gears.
- I love the power of the acceleration.
- I love the control in taking whatever route I want.
- I love the sense of pride in keeping my car in mint
  condition.

So when I contemplate the possibility that a time will come when I shouldn't be driving, when my eyesight, motor skills, and reaction time reach the point that I'm endangering others and myself inside and outside the car, I get despondent and depressed. And then I get angry at the prospect of having one of my life's great pleasures taken away from me.

But then I remember the near calamities that my parents experienced.

While wintering in Arizona, Mom came home from shopping one day with the entire right side of the car ripped up. She had no idea how it happened or that it had even occurred. It turned out that her rapidly escalating and undiagnosed Alzheimer's played a central role.

And early one summer morning in Michigan, Dad, whose MS was causing vivid hallucinations, sneaked out at 4 a.m. to take a spin to his favorite park. Once there, he couldn't remember how to get home, so he (fortunately) waited for us to come find him. It made for a frantic four hours for the rest of the family.

Rather than put our family in those situations, I've decided to establish criteria with my wife and daughter that will help me transition out of the driver's seat. We've even put it in writing to avoid any misunderstanding on their part or backsliding on mine. I've agreed, as part of my yearly physical, to get a thorough eye exam that meets driver's license requirements and to take a test for motor skills and mental acuity.

In addition, we've included an amendment to our agreement that recognizes that tests for visual, physical, and mental dexterity aren't enough.

There can be complications from diabetes that may affect driving and create cognitive problems (that is, does the person forget how to make a left turn?), including dementia.

Further, prescription drugs that I may be taking could also have side effects on my driving ability. At a minimum, these qualitative issues, as well as my annual physical quantitative measures, will be part of our annual Other Talk.

Will I miss zipping around in my sports car when the time comes to become a full-time passenger? You bet.

But I also know that establishing this trigger point now and sharing it with my family will be far easier than scaring them into a "taking away the car keys" confrontation because of some crazy or even lethal driving stunt that I inadvertently performed.

Step 4. Adopt a Comfortable Tone

Now that you have thought through the emotional barriers for each of the participants and have created a structure that will bring the family together, you are ready to develop the atmosphere.

Of course, each family will approach the Other Talk in its own way and on its own terms. But I have found that the most productive and comfortable conversations occurred when the parents had spent time creating a welcoming and involving environment for their kids.

You will want to create a context with a number of dimensions:

- **Informal.** To reduce potential angst and paralysis in your children, it's important that you position the Other Talk as a relaxed, thoughtful, wide-ranging dialogue on a variety of issues that lie ahead.

- **Informative.** Allow family members to engage in an open, honest discussion that clears away potential misunderstandings and wrong assumptions that could result in festering resentments and financial missteps down the road.

- **Collaborative.** The Other Talk is about the rest of your life, not just the end of it. Use this unique opportunity to explore how you want to live your life and what experiences you want to share with your kids as it unfolds.

- **Productive.** Stay focused on results. The more you and your kids anticipate potential twists and turns before infirmities set in, the more likely it is that all of you will navigate those last years with skill, creativity, and confidence.

- **Loving.** Make sure the Other Talk strikes a balance between taking care of business and performing an act of love and affection for your kids.

- **Empowering.** Recognize that while the Other Talk is about you, it also offers a number of life lessons that could benefit your kids in their own lives. It teaches them to be flexible and adaptable as things change in unexpected ways. It enables them to make the tough decisions if and when you can't. It establishes a template from which they can discuss, explore, educate, and think about end-of-life issues with their own children. It demonstrates that "taking care of the kids after I'm gone" isn't just a financial issue. And it adds a dimension to your family relationship that most kids will never know.

In essence, the Other Talk is designed to break the typical eldercare pattern of lurching from one crisis to the next. It gives your kids the self-confidence, knowledge, tools, and perspective to take on the responsibility when the role-reversal process begins to take place.

More important, by preparing for the decisions, the possibilities, and the responsibilities in the last years of your life, you and your kids can focus on the living to be done, the accomplishments that have yet to be achieved, and the memory and the legacy that will make the family proud.

Next Steps

To help you set the stage for your own Other Talk, I'd like to suggest a conceptual and a practical approach:

The Concept of Staging

In preparing for my first Other Talk with my family (Pam, Dakota, and Fernando), I found it helpful to picture myself as the director of an actual on-stage performance.

1. **Preparing the actors.** To begin with, I feel it's important to ensure that the participants develop a thorough understanding of why we're doing this. To answer the Why question, I asked everyone to read the first four chapters of this book:

   - "Defining the Dimensions of the Other Talk"
   - "Recognizing the Negative Consequences of Silence"
   - "Appreciating the Benefits of Family Collaboration"
   - "Navigating the Baby Boomers' Perfect Storm"

2. **Presenting the storyline.** I believe there are three components to effectively communicating and motivating your participants:

- **Engage.** Grab your audience's attention for your concept in a meaningful way.
- **Inform.** Provide information but also ideas and perceptions that will help your audience embrace your concept.
- **Involve.** Keep up your audience's stamina if you want to sustain their attention.

3. **Creating the screenplay.** To guide the participants to the How, you need to provide them with the words and the props. In our case, I created a binder of information, strategies, and contacts for each of our family members. (I'll be discussing that effort in the next chapter.)

4. **Visualizing a successful performance.** I have found it useful, whether it be for sports, writing, public speaking, or even bridge and chess, to imagine a desirable outcome. For the Other Talk, I asked myself to visualize success for two scenarios:

- What will a comfortable, open dialogue look like?
- How will the kids express their interest and commitment to moving forward?

The Practical Approach to Partnership

Of course, setting the stage for the Other Talk is not just about taking into account the mental state of the participants and thinking through the atmospherics of that first get-together.

Because the Other Talk is about establishing a partnership, I encourage you to set ground rules to ensure that this family meeting works smoothly and effectively with a minimum of misunderstanding.

Here's how my family approached those ground rules:

1. You are the managing director; after all, it's your life.
2. The kids are full partners, not corporate minions, because after all their involvement is voluntary.
3. Each member of the partnership (including you) understands that responsibilities will change as your condition evolves.
4. The goals of the partnership are these:

    - To frame decisions now, before a crisis, to ensure better outcomes, less panic and stress, and almost no flailing around
    - To manage your affairs the way you intended and avoid choices you don't want
    - To ensure that everybody benefits and everybody contributes

CHAPTER SIX

Getting Your Documents in Order

I help organize people's lives for a living. But often I find my clients falling short, not in advising their families where to find the necessary documents but rather in explaining why certain decisions were made in instruments like wills and trusts and real estate distributions. This oversight (or cop-out) can be devastating to the family down the road.

—Carly, Certified Financial Planner

When you sit down with your kids to have the Other Talk, a number of key questions will likely come up. As a result, you will want to prepare yourself to address them intelligently and be able to discuss them at some length—questions like these:

- Do your will or trust, living will, and powers of attorney (financial and medical) exist, and are they up to date?
- What key elements and strategies of your financial plan are designed to ensure that you don't outlive your money?
- Is your inventory of documents, family advisors and their phone numbers, safety deposit box locations, and insurance policies readily available?
- Have you made any prearrangements for a funeral service, including personal preferences, instructions, and payments?

The bottom line is that you should plan to spend some time *before* the Other Talk collating and organizing a variety of documents that will give your kids a snapshot of your current situation. This will also provide them with ready access to legal documents if you become incapacitated or when you reach that last sentence.

Don't Procrastinate Because You Feel Overwhelmed

I have one caveat before you start accumulating documents.

It will become clear from reviewing the following pages that finding or requesting or generating the proper up-to-date documentation will most likely be a time-consuming and, at times, frustrating process. What I *don't* want you to do is to put off the Other Talk until you get every last scrap of paper organized, duplicated, and bound into a notebook for each child.

Those notebooks (either paper or electronic) need to be produced because until you put everything together, you have not fully armed your kids to take on the various responsibilities in your last years. But the notebook is not the goal; it is merely a means to an end.

As you begin the accumulation process, I want you to stay focused on one singular objective: the more information your kids have, and the sooner they get it, the better for you and for them.

That's why you need to commit yourself and your family, right here, right now, to having the Other Talk within the next three months with as much documentation as you can pull together.

Waiting until the binders are complete is just another form of procrastination, one with potentially serious consequences. Here's how Darlene, a senior marketing executive, described the price she and her sisters ended up paying:

> By the time we found out how sick Mom was, she went into a coma. We had no idea if she had a will, a living will, or powers of attorney, or if she did, where to find them. We had no clue about her financial dealings or situation. So we were flying blind, having to make all the decisions for her.

When you've got all this illness thrust on you all at once, the pressure to make the right calls (the ones Mom would have wanted but never told us) and the need to take on the day-to-day responsibilities become truly overwhelming.

What Could Go into Your Notebooks?

With that in mind, it's time to get to work. The list of documents described in the next few pages is not intended to be definitive, nor does it represent expert advice. You should talk with your financial, legal, and accounting advisors about how to meet your individual needs.

But this list *is* designed to get you started thinking about the wealth of information you need to prepare and bring to the Other Talk. Further, you will want to review and update these documents annually for the subsequent Other Talks to reflect changes in your assets and in your preferences.

The Will or Trust

An original will or trust is the most important document you need to keep on file. You need to let your kids know where it is located, and I would strongly recommend that you share it with them now to avoid misunderstandings, resentments, and legal actions after you're gone.

A will or trust allows you to dictate how your estate will be handled and who will inherit your assets, which will simplify or avoid the probate process. Further, not having the original document means that family members can challenge your wishes in court.

Medical Information

1. **Advance directives.** There are two key advance directive documents that you will want to fill out and give to your kids at the Other Talk:

   - A *durable healthcare power of attorney*, which allows your designee to make healthcare decisions on your behalf if you are incapacitated
   - A *living will*, which details your wishes at the end of life, often including a "do not resuscitate" (DNR) order

     You should also give these advance directives to your primary care doctor so the directives can be included in your medical record. Further, if you have scheduled surgery or other planned hospital admissions, you should bring copies with you to make it part of your medical chart.

2. **Doctors.** You will want to create a summary list of all of your doctors and other medical advisors that includes their names and contact information, medical specialty, a brief description of your diagnosis, and the treatment plan and timeline.

3. **Medications.** You need to develop a list of
   prescription and nonprescription medications that
   includes the type and strength of each medication,
   what the medication is treating, where to obtain
   prescription refills (pharmacy or mail order),
   and the name of the physician who wrote the
   prescription.

Financial Information

You need to provide contact information for key advisors
(attorney, financial planner, accountant, stockbroker, real
estate agent, etc.). Your kids will need the name, address,
phone and fax numbers, and e-mail address for each of these
individuals.

Key Documents

Your family needs to know where to find a variety of documents (the originals and copies if applicable) because your
kids won't be able to make decisions or take actions on your
behalf without them. These documents include your birth
certificate, Social Security card, marriage license, passport,
trust documents, and, if applicable, a divorce judgment and
decree, or the stipulation agreement if settled out of court.

Insurance for Life, Health, Home, Vehicles, and Boats

Provide family members with the name of the carrier, the
policy number, policy type and specifics, and the agent con-

nected with each policy. Be sure to include any life or health policies granted by a company upon retirement.

The availability of this information is critical, especially for life insurance, since insurers are not required to determine whether a policyholder has died. As a result, a claim is paid only when the surviving family members contact the company.

This nonpayment of claims is a bigger problem than you might think. More than $400 million in unclaimed life insurance payments have piled up between 2000 and 2011 in the state of New York alone, according to the New York state comptroller's office.

Tax Returns

The kids will need to know the location of your most recent seven years of returns. This is necessary for IRS queries, but it is also helpful, when the time comes, in determining the extent of assets in the estate and in filing a final income tax and estate return and, if applicable, a revocable trust return.

Banking Information

Your family needs the location, names on accounts, account numbers, and contact information for each of your checking and savings accounts, as well as the location and contents of your safety deposit box. Be sure to register your spouse's and kids' names with the bank, and have them sign the registration document so they can gain access without a court order.

Proofs of Ownership

You need to accumulate in a central location the original documentation of housing and land ownership deeds, cemetery plots, vehicle and boat titles, savings bonds, and partnership or corporate operating agreements.

Investment, Pension, and Loan Information

Your heirs will need to know the location of an inventory of current investments, including taxable and traditional and Roth IRA accounts and your 401(k) and 403(b) plans, plus the account numbers and the contact information for who handles each.

You should also let your kids know where to find your latest statement from Social Security; company pension plan details and contact information; original mortgage and any home equity loans and most recent refinancing details; a summary of the loans you have outstanding and the repayment terms; and a summary of the debts you owe. (Wills and living trusts should be written to direct how debts are to be settled.)

Credit Card Information

You should copy the front and back of all active credit cards and indicate the location of the most recent statements, especially if there are outstanding balances.

Valuable Items Information

You will want to provide your family with a summary of antiques, jewelry, original artwork, family heirlooms, and any other valuables, along with the most current appraisals.

Burial and Funeral Information

Certainly your kids will want to honor your wishes at the end of life. That's why you need to summarize your choices on these aspects:

- Cremation or burial
- Type of service (such as where, what kind, who will preside, visitation, specific music and/or readings, military proceedings)
- Organ donation arrangements and time frame
- Location of burial plot and type of grave marker
- Charity donation in lieu of flowers

In addition, you will want to let your kids know if you have prepaid for a funeral service or taken out burial insurance, and with whom. Just like the life insurance companies, these prepaid providers are under no obligation to contact the family, and they will pocket the proceeds if no request is made. (This actually happened to my family, even though both parents had paid in full.)

To conclude, I want to encourage you to schedule the Other Talk within the next three months with as much documentation as you can pull together.

Since there will undoubtedly be information gaps that will need to be filled in, however, I'd ask you to add to your preliminary notebook a page that lays out a timetable for its completion. Only then have you fully prepared your kids to take on the various responsibilities as your last years unfold.

The more information your kids have and the sooner they get it, the better for you and for them.

Next Steps

Bringing all this information, strategies, and contacts together in a binder is critical to a successful Other Talk. But it isn't just about the accumulation of data that this binder represents. It is also important to use it to establish a framework and a goal orientation to the process.

First, it presents a rare opportunity for your family to come together to talk about what's important to you, to sit back and think about what life has meant to you, what you would like to accomplish next, and what you would like to leave behind as your memory—your legacy.

Second, by having a thoughtful and wide-ranging dialogue *before* infirmities set in, your family can create a road map that will help them realize some of those aspirations.

Third, it can lead your family down the path to an open, honest conversation that clears away the underbrush of misunderstandings and wrong assumptions that often can result in resentments, anxieties, and financial missteps.

Fourth, the more you and your kids anticipate potential twists and turns, the more likely it is that all of you will navigate those last years with skill and confidence.

PART THREE

Turning the Other Talk into an Action Plan

························

When I finally got around to asking Mom to sign the financial power of attorney document, she refused. She had apparently reached a point where she just didn't trust anybody. Her fear was, "If I do this, you'll throw me out on the street. I'm giving up all this stuff that I've had all my life." To her it looked like I had gone too far, like I was trying to pull a fast one.

—Norman, focus group participant

CHAPTER SEVEN

Financing Your Uncertain Future

I wish I had known what the rights of trustees were in advance, that they get to decide what funds are liquidated when and that they are represented by counsel, who is paid for out of the estate. I also discovered that one sibling can waste a lot of the trustee's time and accordingly draw down on the estate with constant arguing and stonewalling.

—Margie, focus group participant

One of the most complex and daunting challenges that we face as we get older is trying to figure out how to manage our money in the last years of life. The problem, quite simply, is that the ending (when, where, and how) as well as the associated costs are unknowable.

Sadly, many people deal with this financial conundrum the same way they approach other challenges in the last years of life: with healthy doses of procrastination and inertia.

In fact, it has been estimated that 53 percent of Americans 25 and older haven't even *tried* to calculate how much they will need to save to live comfortably in retirement, according to a March 2013 study by the Employee Benefit Research Institute.

Yet despite inaction by so many, it's a problem that is top of mind for most Americans. More than 81 percent of respondents to a *Consumer Reports* survey said that they worry about being able to afford healthcare in retirement, and 68 percent worry that they'll go bankrupt paying for medical bills following a serious illness or accident.

Even wealthier people seem frozen in the headlights. Two-thirds of people with at least $250,000 in investable assets expressed concern that they would outlive their retirement nest egg, according to a 2011 study by Bank of America Merrill Lynch.

Unfortunately, this fear of running out of money in your last years, in particular due to overwhelming medical expenses, is not misplaced. A 2009 *American Journal of Medicine* article reported that 62 percent of personal bankruptcies are caused by medical problems.

I don't know about you, but I was stunned by this statistic. Then, as I began looking into the likely causes of this financial catastrophe, I realized that the Other Talk could play a significant role in overcoming the inertia over retirement planning while also directly addressing the worry of outlasting your assets.

The Leading Drivers of Financial Problems at the End of Life

The first driver is what the medical profession calls the "compression of morbidity." The layperson's translation of this rather gruesome terminology is that the bulk of an individual's spending on healthcare will occur in that person's last two years, and especially the last six months.

In other words, morbidity—the incidence of various illnesses—accelerates at the end of life, with multiple medical specialists getting into the act. This can become very costly, and it is the reason that Medicare now spends nearly one-third of its total budget on patients in their last 12 months of life.

The second cause of financial problems at the end of life is that our expectations don't come close to reflecting reality, as can be seen in the following table, which was part of a 2010 TIAA-CREF study:

Retirement Expectations

	PERCEPTION	REALITY
MY SPENDING IN RETIREMENT WILL:		
DECREASE	56%	36%
STAY THE SAME	36%	47%
INCREASE	8%	22%

This analysis shows that 56 percent of people in the study believed that their spending would decrease in retirement. The reality was that spending decreased for only 31 percent of respondents. At the other end, only 8 percent of people in the study expected their spending to increase in their retirement. In reality, 22 percent of respondents saw their spending increase during this time.

The implication is that you will likely spend a lot more money in retirement than your financial assumptions have allowed for.

Finally, elderly parents can get in trouble because they lose the mental capacity to control their finances.

Ralph, who was in one of my focus groups, remembered standing by helplessly, watching his 82-year-old mother drive her financial wagon off a cliff:

> She kept living like there was no tomorrow. She kept spending and spending and spending like she had it, except she didn't. Piling up debt on credit cards, buying cars she didn't need, continually overdrawing her bank account.
>
> It was a nightmare, but I didn't know how to stop her.

How can you explicitly deal with the causes of financial ruin: the potential healthcare train wreck in the last year or so of life, the tendency to spend too much before you realize that you are not controlling your finances as capably as you once did?

Essentially, you need a plan—not a static one, but a dynamic one that includes your spouse and your kids, who will be instrumental in implementing it.

In my view, coming up with a singular "number" is a good start, but considering it the answer to retirement planning is naive and potentially dangerous. Just ask the families who went bankrupt in the last years of their parents' lives because of unplanned medical expenses.

What you need is the dynamism of the Other Talk, which is about managing evolution in your last years of life and addressing decision making, roles and responsibilities, asset management, living arrangements, and healthcare needs.

What you need is the adaptability and flexibility inherent in the Other Talk process, which you can achieve by committing to annual updates. This will ensure that you and your family revisit your assumptions and financial condition so that you can recalibrate your plan if the current reality requires it.

Finally, what you need to remember is that the Other Talk isn't just about the orderly distribution of your assets while you're alive and when you are gone. It's also a means to an end: how to get the most out of the rest of your life and how to involve your kids in that adventure.

Discussing How to Finance
Your Uncertain Future

Fundamentally, this financial part of the Other Talk should be focused on a series of what-if scenarios because your situation in your last years is forever fluid.

Physically, your condition will evolve, requiring various levels and types of medical care. Social Security and Medicare benefits may change; tax rates and policies may be rewritten. Real estate valuations can reverse course (remember when conventional wisdom held that housing prices would never go down?). And the investment environment can be volatile. Conventional wisdom had it that stocks in the long term would increase in value, yet between 2000 and 2010 the Dow Jones Industrial Average barely moved upward, although it had very volatile ups and downs in that period.

Establishing Your Spending Priorities

As a result, in preparing for the "financing your uncertain future" discussion, I recommend that you bring a contingency planning mindset as you ponder the guiding principles of this conversation: What is the life you want? What is the life you don't want? What are the costs of each?

To answer these questions, you need to establish a clear picture of your financial situation, develop a series of what-if scenarios that demonstrate what you want to accomplish and experience, and then determine how realistically these various scenarios can exist within your financial reality.

For example, the life you want may be three overseas trips every year, plus a house in the country. The life you don't want may be living in a nursing home and giving up driving your car. When you run the numbers, however, you realize that the costs of international travel, a second home, eventual 24/7 care in your home, and a car will consume your assets by age 71. You need to revisit the life you want and the one you don't want.

Or perhaps you have approached the aspirations of your last years more qualitatively: I want my life to be busy, useful, flexible, relevant. I want to be always learning and physically active.

Of course, there are a number of ways to achieve those goals, each at different price points. Your job then is to pick and choose those that meet your budget.

However you think about the life you want, either quantitatively or qualitatively, I would recommend one more level of contingency planning. To maximize the fun and satisfaction in your last years, consider setting goals and priorities by decade. For example:

- Adventure travel, like climbing the Inca Trail to Machu Picchu, in your sixties
- Guided tours, like bike trips in the Michigan countryside, in your seventies
- Theater and museum trips in your eighties
- Extreme bingo in your nineties

Certainly, your health and wealth will dictate whether your timetable speeds up or slows down, but at least you won't be waiting to strike out on some adventure until it's too late for you physically or financially.

Perhaps the most important thing to keep in mind as you consider your dreams, goals, and aspirations is that the path to true happiness is enjoying what you have: family, health, and whatever resources you've accumulated.

Creating Your Retirement Income Plan

Whichever approach you take to your spending priorities, you're not finished yet. You need to bring that same what-if mindset to your assets and your budget because the world is not a static place and neither is your pile of money.

Social Security

When should you start taking Social Security? This is one of the most critical decisions that you need to make because your timing will affect not only your net worth but also your spending plans throughout your retirement years.

Past conventional wisdom held that it was best to take benefits early (for today's 60-somethings that would be age 66) and to invest the proceeds. Of course, another reason to claim Social Security at 66, or even as early as 62, is if you're in ill health or have a family history of early mortality—or if you simply need the money.

But experts today recommend waiting as long as you can to receive your benefits. Waiting until age 70 to collect means your monthly payment could increase by as much as 32 percent.

Available Retirement Benefits

If you are a military veteran, check with the U.S. Department of Veterans Affairs to see if you are eligible for a veterans pension and other benefits.

In addition, the National Council on Aging has identified more than 2,000 different programs that can assist elders with long-term care as well as subsidies for food, medication, and housing. Check out www.benefitscheckup.org for a complete listing.

Savings

Finally, you need to analyze your nest egg to determine whether you will outlive it or vice versa. To make this determination, consider a number of variables that not too many years ago made this exercise a daunting and imprecise task but that today are readily available.

Generating Financial Projections

Fortunately, in this age of computer modeling, creating what-if scenarios has become fairly easy and straightforward. Software programs, often offered free of charge by brokerages, insurance companies, and financial planners, can help you generate a series of financial projections, each based on various spending assumptions and investment strategies.

Personal Data for the Projections

Of course, you are going to need to do your homework because your what-if projections are only as good as the accuracy of the data you provide. Depending on the software you are using, you'll need to accumulate this type of information:

Annual Expenses

- Essential expenses
- Discretionary expenses (such as travel, dining out, entertainment, and clothes)
- Supplemental healthcare insurance
- Long-term healthcare insurance

Income

- Social Security
- Salary, bonus, and other work-related (earned) income
- 401(k), 403(b), and IRA accounts
- Pension benefits
- Annuity income
- Other income (such as dividends, interest, rental income, and real estate sales including your home)

Current Assets

- Investment portfolio, including the dollar amount and percentage of total for stocks, bonds, and short-term instruments
- Real estate
- Other assets (such as antiques and artwork)
- Level of risk you are comfortable with

Depending on the software program, you may be able to project the future value of your assets against various market performance assumptions. More important, you may be able to estimate when your assets will be fully depleted.

What-If Scenarios

Armed with these data, you can start working what-if scenarios. For example:

- What happens if I change my retirement date?
- What happens if I change our annual spending rate?
- What happens if I change our asset mix?
- What happens if I convert from owning to renting?

Revisiting Your Retirement Plan

Finally, these software programs are useful not only in estimating an end date for your nest egg but also in encouraging you to revisit key decisions such as the following in your own personal retirement plan:

- How long will you and your spouse live? According to an analysis by the Society of Actuaries, there is a 25 percent chance that a 65-year-old in good health will live to 92 if male, 94 if female, and 97 if he or she is a surviving spouse from a married couple.
- Can your investment portfolio at least match the rate of inflation?
- Have you established a withdrawal rate that won't jeopardize your long-term future?
- Have you set aside funds to supplement Medicare and cover out-of-pocket healthcare costs, which Fidelity Investments estimate at $220,000 for a couple aged 65, one of whom lives to 92?
- Do you want to leave an inheritance for your kids, or is your goal like René's, one of my research respondents: "I want the last check that I write before I die to bounce!"

Planning for Role Reversal

Now that you've run due diligence on your financial plan, both spending priorities and the ability of your nest egg to deliver on them for *all* of your last years, it's time for you and your spouse to take one more step before you're ready to sit down with the family to have the Other Talk.

The two of you need to put a mechanism in place that shifts financial responsibilities from you to your kids with as little drama as possible. By building that mechanism with your children now, it will look and feel like (and will in fact be) prudent planning, rather than a fight over financial control.

If you postpone action, thinking, "I'll know when it's time," you will most likely find yourself out of the loop, losing your ability to guide an effective transition because either a sudden disability happened so fast that the rules of the game changed before you could react or creeping dementia sneaked up on you.

About half of Americans in their eighties have some form of dementia or cognitive decline. But problems usually start well before that, as noted in a 2010 study that appeared in the *Wall Street Journal*. According to the study by George Korniotis of the Federal Reserve and Alok Kumar of the University of Texas business school, recent research into our financial decision-making skills suggests they begin to slip after age 70 and suffer more rapid declines after 75, much as aging athletes lose speed and agility. As a result, your mental decline will be incremental, most likely so gradual that you won't even notice (although those around you increasingly will). So, like the over-the-hill athlete who refuses to leave the game, you'll insist on maintaining your position until your kids are forced to drag you off the field.

Nobody wins that one. So let's consider the Other Talk approach.

Step 1. Establish a Financial Power of Attorney

If you have more than one child and all or some of them will be participating in the Other Talk, I recommend dividing up the responsibilities among them:

- One child could oversee the finances and handle all the bill paying.
- Another could monitor the medical diagnoses and treatments and stay on top of doctor visits.
- A third could be in charge of the home maintenance or be the liaison with the assisted-living center.

That way all the kids have a responsibility, nobody feels over-burdened and eventually underappreciated, and the opportunities for sibling disagreements are reduced.

When choosing the child who will handle your finances (I'll get to the other two choices in later chapters), Linda Kaare, a Michigan elder-law attorney, urges that you should select "someone who is organized, dependable, and trustworthy and is financially stable in his or her own life."

In addition, you should be honest about the amount of work and the challenges involved. When it came time for me to take over the financial responsibilities for my parents, I found the tasks—paying bills, making investment decisions, and filing tax returns, to name a few—fairly time-consuming and ongoing, especially since my parents and I lived in different states.

There are shortcuts, however, like electronic banking and automatic withdrawals for recurring expenses, like home healthcare, utilities, and phone bills, which will save time and allow the kids to monitor your accounts for correct deposits and withdrawals.

In addition, keeping an eye on the money can help your kids protect you from financial scams that target older Americans, which have become so prevalent that the National Council on Aging, on its website, calls them the crime of the century:

> Why? Because seniors are thought to have a significant amount of money sitting in their accounts. Financial scams also often go unreported or can be difficult to prosecute, so they're considered a low-risk crime.
>
> However, they are devastating to many older adults and can leave them in a very vulnerable position with little time to recoup their losses.

Here's just one example from National Council on Aging's top-10 list of scams that illustrates how easy it is for someone in the last years of life to be separated from his or her money:

> The Grandparent Scam is so simple and so underhanded, because it uses one of older adults' most reli-

able assets, their hearts. Scammers will place a call to an older person, and when the mark picks up, they will say something along the lines of, "Hi, Grandma, do you know who this is?" When the unsuspecting grandparent guesses the name of the grandchild the scammer most sounds like, the scammer has established a fake identity without having done a lick of background research.

Once "in," the fake grandchild will usually ask for money to solve some unexpected financial problem (overdue rent, payment for car repairs, etc.), to be paid via Western Union or MoneyGram, which don't always require identification to collect. At the same time, the scam artist will beg the grandparent, "Please don't tell my parents; they would kill me."

Once you have settled on which of your children you want to help you manage the finances *and* that child has agreed to take on that responsibility, you need to make your choice known to the family. Then you should move on three fronts, and I urge you to act quickly.

Documentation

To begin, you should execute a *financial power of attorney*, which is basically a written, signed, and notarized document through which the parents give the designated child the authority to manage the parents' money—the right to do everything from writing checks to selling securities. Powers of attorney can be effective immediately or upon incapacity. Unfortunately, it seems that assigning a financial power of attorney is an easy task to procrastinate. In a 1991 survey, nearly three-quarters of Americans 45 years and older said they hadn't gotten around to it, according to AARP.

Because you can write your own definition of "incapacity," I would strongly encourage you to get to this document as soon as possible. The most common definition requires two physicians to declare the person incapacitated.

Power of attorney documents are usually drafted by lawyers, but they don't have to be. You can find templates on Internet websites, some of which are listed in the Appendix "Online Resources for the Other Talk."

Financial Assistance

Sit all your kids down for face-to-face meetings with your financial advisors: banker, lawyer, broker, accountant, insurance agent, financial planner, and any others as needed. The purpose is to get acquainted in preparation for future dealings and for everyone concerned to understand your financial strategies and tactics, as well as how things have been set up.

If you don't currently use advisors, then when you first get together for the Other Talk, you should discuss with your kids the pros and cons of getting financial assistance. You may decide that outsourcing some of your financial decision making and execution may provide your family with useful expertise while also reducing familial friction and leaving time for all of you to do other things.

Asset Distribution

The third point to make with your kids, especially the one handling the finances, is that under current U.S. law, spouses who are U.S. citizens can pass unlimited assets to each other, either during their lifetime or after death. Distributing assets to other beneficiaries, however, including the children, is subject to certain limitations. To understand the rules, your family should consult with a tax and/or financial planning expert.

Step 2. Simplify Your Finances

As you probably discovered when you began to put together the notebooks that I discussed in Chapter 6, "Getting Your Documents in Order," you've got stuff all over the place. While the notebook technique enables you to consolidate all your financial matters physically, I would also ask you to simplify your finances structurally as well. For example:

- Have your monthly checks (such as dividends, annuities, and pensions) deposited automatically. (Your Social Security payment is probably already automatically deposited.)
- Put as many bills as possible on autopay (including utilities, memberships, house of worship pledges, and ongoing charity donations).

- Consolidate your checking and savings accounts to one bank.
- Transfer investment holdings, including IRAs, profit sharing, and 401(k) and 403(b) accounts, to a single financial services company.

The bottom line is that the more you put on autopilot, the better off you will be as you move into your seventies, eighties, and beyond. For certain, the kid you designated your financial power of attorney will appreciate you for it.

Step 3. Transfer the Roles Between Your Spouse or Partner and You

In preparation for discussing financial role reversal in the Other Talk, one area that often gets overlooked is the potential need to shift responsibilities from one spouse to another if one becomes incapacitated or dies. You'll want to prepare for this.

Let's say you have been handling the bill paying and your partner has been the hands-on investor as your nest egg began to grow.

You should give your partner a tutorial and possibly a road map of the payment process (such as autopay, e-mail, and mail); the monthly budget, if it exists; and the location where the receipts are kept.

Your partner should provide you with a detailed summary of what financial resources are available (and hopefully that summary is housed in the Other Talk binder by now), and he or she should walk through the what-if scenarios in the plan discussed earlier in this chapter.

Once you've both been briefed on each other's roles, you should determine the trigger points that will prompt the other partner to take over. Since this transfer of roles likely means that one partner is taking on both bill paying and investing, he or she should determine the following:

- How much responsibility to retain personally
- How much to pass on to the kids
- How much to turn over to an outside expert

Since these determinations will have important implications for the kids, they should be made part of the Other Talk.

Next Steps

We've just spent an entire chapter on ways to manage your money *during* your last years of life. Our financial planning story won't be complete, however, until we deal with steps to be taken to avoid financial hassles *after* the death of a parent or a spouse.

Create a Password Library Card

In this increasingly digital world we live in (and depend on), it is no longer good enough to leave just a safety deposit box key with your spouse and kids for when you pass on.

Quite simply, many of your documents and your protocols for accessing your assets probably aren't housed in that box. Most likely, a lot of the really important stuff is sitting on your hard drive inside your computer.

As a result, you need to create a password library card, then find a secure place for it—definitely not your computer but perhaps in your safety deposit box.

On the card be sure to list your log-in and/or user name, password, and other prompts, such as your answers to security questions, for as many electronic relationships as you can think of, including these:

- E-mail accounts
- Computers
- Social media accounts
- Online accounts for retailers
- Online accounts for ongoing bill paying (for example, utilities, mortgage, and charities)
- Frequent-flyer accounts
- Tablets, music players, and digital readers

Establish Joint Ownership

One layer of grief you don't want to lay on your surviving spouse or kids is locking up your assets because they're only in your name. Your family could spend months and lots of legal fees trying to gain access to funds that they may need in the short term.

It would make sense and be relatively easy if you go back to the binder that I discussed in Chapter 6 and make sure that all your assets (including your checking account) are in joint ownership with your spouse or partner and that your listed beneficiaries are up to date.

Unwind Joint Accounts . . . Carefully

On the subject of joint checking accounts, I have heard a number of horror stories of surviving spouses' automatically taking the deceased's name off the account, only to then be locked out of the account. There's no rush to make the name adjustment, so get to it when you have less on your plate and can check with the bank on the best way to go about it.

For retirement accounts, the standard advice is to roll over the deceased's account into your own. But if you, the surviving spouse, are under 59½, withdrawals from the consolidated IRA will trigger a 10 percent penalty.

Better to consider an "inherited IRA," which, if the deceased was younger than 70½, allows the surviving spouse to withdraw without penalty. Withdrawals must begin the year that the deceased would have hit 70½. (Check all this out with your accountant since things change—this is not meant to be financial advice.)

CHAPTER EIGHT

Selecting the Best Living Arrangement

If anybody were going to "put me" in a nursing home and I had any mental capacity, I wouldn't want to be "put," so I almost hope for some benign neglect on my daughter's part.

—Athena, focus group participant

The desire of most Americans to live in their own home throughout their last years is powerful and deep-seated. According to AARP, 90 percent of people older than 65 prefer to remain in their home. And 90 percent of people, if they had less than six months to live, would choose limited care at home rather than advanced medical intervention in a hospital or nursing home, according to a 1992 Gallup poll.

This preference shouldn't be surprising since there are a number of real benefits to living at home. You'll spend your days in a familiar setting (perhaps where your children grew up, with the many pleasant memories that contains), surrounded by your "things" (family heirlooms, furniture, and other possessions that you bought with or for your spouse, kids' playthings, and artwork). You'll remain near your friends and family, your social network, your neighborhood, your favorite stores and restaurants, and places of entertainment and worship. And you'll retain feelings of independence, control, predictability, and self-esteem.

Then there's the flip side of this strongly held desire to live out your days at home, which is the gruesome image of the traditional alternative: the nursing home.

Many people think of nursing homes as rather grim places where the residents shuffle about or sit in front of the television feeling bored, lonely, sad, and helpless.

For my great-uncle Virgil, a nursing home was the stark reminder of his mortality:

The only thing wrong with this place is that we're all old. We look around and are reminded of what we used to be and the things we can't do anymore. It's depressing.

For others, moving into a nursing home is often seen as a sign of failure, as observed by Elinor Ginzler, former director of livable communities for AARP, in a marketwatch.com article.

It means that they can no longer live independently, that they have diminished capabilities. Not surprisingly, many seniors go through a grieving process when deciding to move or when moving into an assisted-living facility.

It's the same sort of grief that one experiences with the loss of a loved one.

Perhaps the harshest, although often accurate, indictment comes from Dr. William Thomas, a leading proponent of nursing home reform and the creator of the Green House Project, which has redesigned the nursing home concept to give residents more privacy and more control over their lives:

I believe that in [nursing homes] in America, every year, thousands and thousands of people die of a broken heart. They die not so much because their organs fail but because their grip on life has failed.

The reality is that many facilities are much better than this dreary image. Further, new concepts have been and are being developed that go beyond the traditional "warehouse for the aging" approach.

One example is called a *continuing care retirement community* (CCRC), which provides various levels of healthcare at one location. You generally start in *independent living*, where you move into your own apartment when you are healthy and don't need personal assistance. The next level is *assisted living*, which you can access when you need a little help with the activities of daily living, like bathing and getting to the dining room. Finally, you can move into *skilled nursing and rehabilitation* when you require round-the-clock monitoring and treatment.

While this approach can prove beneficial for anyone in his or her last years, it is particularly appealing to couples because it allows one spouse to receive a different level of care while allowing the two of them to continue socializing, dining, and being together.

A Recipe for Disaster

But no matter how enlightened and homelike the facility, the most typical path to nursing home care is unpleasant: the parent suffers a health crisis. The family has 48 hours or less to explore options before the patient discharge. The parent is placed into a nursing home without discussion.

Because the decision to move the parent out of the house and into an institution occurred in the midst of a crisis, it's a recipe for disaster. Here's how Sarah Wells, executive director of the National Consumer Voice for Quality Long-Term Care, has described it:

It's really difficult when you're faced with a long-term care decision. It can be a time of chaos, often fast and furious.

Since there was no time to talk to or prepare the parent for the move, this short-term solution can easily morph into years of resentment and misery for the parents and kids alike.

Making a Long-Term Care Plan

My point is not to denigrate the value of nursing homes, CCRCs, or other forms of assisted-living facilities. For some people, the level of necessary care these places provide is far better than staying at home. And for others, like my grandmother, it can actually be a liberating experience. Grandma, at age 80, enthusiastically moved out of her house and into a continuing care retirement community *primarily* for the wide range of social interactions and the freedom to travel.

But to avoid your kids' being swept up in the chaotic rush to the first nursing home available, your spouse and you need to make a long-term care plan now. The two of you should have a thorough and realistic conversation about where you want to live in your last years and how that can be accomplished. Then you'll want to make it an important component of the Other Talk because your kids will surely be affected, whether you settle on living at home until the very end, moving to some form of assisted living, living with your kids, or combining all of the above.

As you prepare for this discussion, I would urge you to consider each of these four alternatives thoroughly and dispassionately, rather than emotionally embracing one and building a wall of defense against the other three.

Living at Home Until the Very End

It can be done.

I know, because my two brothers and I, living in different parts of the country, accomplished it for my parents, including the last seven years with Mom in late-stage Alzheimer's and Dad struggling physically and mentally with multiple sclerosis.

It was emotionally draining, thoroughly exhausting, and incredibly time-consuming, mostly because we were making it up as we stumbled along. While at the end of the day we felt a sense of accomplishment in helping Mom and Dad achieve their passion, I know that a healthy dose of preplanning would have made this entire experience a whole lot better for everyone.

So that you can avoid some of our missteps, wrong turns, and dead ends, I will tell you how we would have done it differently, based on our own experience, plus my readings of and discussions with elder care professionals.

Start with a Realistic Picture of Living

I have already talked about the benefits of spending the rest of your days in your home: a familiar setting surrounded by your things; your own friends, family, and neighborhood;

a semblance of predictability; and your independence and self-esteem intact.

Before succumbing to the emotional tug of the living-at-home option, however, you should honestly explore the challenges. As you get older, you will probably eventually need a hand with everyday tasks, like shopping, transportation, cooking, and bathing. As your health ultimately declines, you will need more and more access to healthcare. And as time goes on, the potential dangers of isolation and loneliness become more real, particularly for people with physical or mental disabilities.

You should also add up the obvious and not-so-obvious costs of living at home in your last years: mortgage and/or home equity loan payments; taxes and utilities, including projected increases; gas, maintenance, repairs, and insurance for aging cars and aging drivers; public and/or private transportation; home maintenance and repair projects, since you eventually won't be doing them yourself, if you ever did.

If, after a thorough airing of the pros and cons, you decide that living at home is best for your spouse and you, you will want to take several steps to ensure that you will be happy and secure in your decision.

Design Your Home of the Future

You'll want to start by determining how to modify your home for your later years of life, and how much it will cost. As a result, you will not only be aware of the financial implications of the necessary modifications but you'll also avoid the all-too-common strategy of, "I'll make those changes after I fall and break my hip."

Of course, this careful evaluation of your surroundings is important whether you elect to remain in your current home, downsize to a more manageable property, or migrate to another house somewhere else.

The basic concept in designing your home for your latter years is called *universal design*, which means the users of the space and their needs dictate the most effective layout of the living quarters. In your case, the goal is to maintain functional status as long as possible by focusing on comfort, accessibility, and safety.

Essentially, you will be modifying your home for decreasing mobility and sensory issues.

The good news is that while some of the changes—like moving the master bedroom and full bathroom to the first floor, installing multilevel countertops in the kitchen and bathroom, or building an outdoor ramp—may prove costly, many of the alterations you can accomplish yourself while you are still active, or you can have them done for you, at a modest cost.

If you are thinking about remodeling your home anytime in the future, you should incorporate universal design into your plans.

Here's a potpourri of basic adjustments to get you thinking about the kinds of modifications you will want to include in your house of the future. Keep in mind that you don't have to perform all these adjustments at once, especially the wheelchair-accessible items, but you *should* have them in your plan.

Finally, here's a suggestion to help you generate your own ideas: borrow or rent a wheelchair for a day; then roll yourself around the house to get a different perspective on comfort, accessibility, and safety.

For a thorough discussion of designing your home for universal access, see AARP's *Home Fit Guide* at www.aarp. org or read AARP's *Guide to Revitalizing Your Home,* www. aarp.org/RevitalizingYourHome.

Throughout the House

- Lever-style door handles: easier to handle than doorknobs, especially when arms are full of packages
- Brighter lighting with adjustable controls: better for aging eyesight
- Handrails on both sides of all steps: easier to navigate
- Double-sided tape or carpet mesh to secure area rugs: helpful in preventing tripping or slipping
- No threshold at the entrance to the home: more wheelchair accessible (and allows wheelchair occupant to enter with dignity and comfort)
- Raised electrical outlets and lowered light switches: more wheelchair accessible
- Strategically placed flashing light attached to doorbell: better for people with hearing impairments

Kitchen

- Under-the-cabinet lighting: better for aging eyesight
- Slide-out drawers: easier access to pots and pans
- D-shaped cabinet and drawer handles versus knobs: easier to grasp

Bathroom

- Strategically placed grab bars in bath and shower (requires reinforcing spaces behind wall): better accessibility and safer
- Bath and shower chairs: more comfortable and convenient
- Lever handles on faucets: easier to handle
- No floor barrier at shower entrance: more accessible

There are a number of professional resources to turn to for help in evaluating your home and determining the most effective and cost-efficient ways to achieve comfort, accessibility, and safety in your home of the future:

- The National Association of Home Builders, in conjunction with AARP, has developed the Certified Aging-in-Place Specialist (CAPS) curriculum and certification to train remodelers in how to design and implement home modifications for seniors.
- Hundreds of nonprofit independent-living centers throughout the country provide services to people with

disabilities. Many offer free assessments of a home's architectural barriers, like steps and narrow doorways.

- A growing number of occupational therapists work with remodelers; many of them have undergone the CAPS training.

Prepare Yourself for Assisted Living at Home

Since you are currently physically active, mentally sharp, and in good health, now is the time to scope out the extra help and services for when you're not, if you are serious about staying in your home. The key is to find good-quality and reliable sources of assistance at different levels of service. Below are a few places you may want to begin your search.

A *home health aide* can provide a variety of nonmedical (but necessary) care services like housekeeping, buying groceries, preparing meals, doing the laundry, taking out the trash, getting you to the doctor, bathing and accomplishing personal hygiene tasks, taking you to a movie or a restaurant, or just sitting and sharing a conversation.

An *adult daycare center* can provide an outlet for social interaction, mental stimulation, or just a place to hang out. Fortunately, many of these places are beginning to recognize that they "need to change the way they do business," according to Constance Todd, director of the National Institute of Senior Centers at the National Council on Aging, as quoted in a 2005 *Boston Globe* article. "That means salads instead of beef stew," officials told the *Globe*, "theatrical productions instead of sing-alongs, fitness classes instead of bingo games, and computer seminars instead of knitting classes."

A *geriatric care manager* can work with you and your family to create a personalized plan that integrates your medical care with your home care, as well as your financial and legal needs. The geriatric care manager then executes the plan by assigning and overseeing the necessary in-home support staff (for example, nurses, social workers, exercise and nutritional specialists, and home health aides), as well as collaborating with your doctors and medical specialists.

Explore Funding Opportunities for Homeowners

Not surprisingly, the various assisted-living services that will help keep you in your home as you age cost money. Hopefully, you have worked through your finances, as discussed in Chapter 7, "Financing Your Uncertain Future," and you will have taken the cost of these home care services into account.

One advantage of staying in your home is that you have some excellent opportunities to fund that lifestyle choice. Below are three possibilities that my brothers and I explored; there are certainly others that may better fit your situation. In any case, you will want financial and legal advice for whatever direction you decide to take.

Reverse Mortgage

This financial instrument allows you to get your equity out without moving out of your home, but experts advise that it is risky.

Advantages: You qualify if you are 62 or older and you own your home free and clear or you owe a small enough amount that it can be paid off with part of your reverse mortgage distribution. How much you can take out depends on your age and the value of the home, among other things. You can take out your equity in a lump sum, as a monthly installment, or as a line of credit. The more you take out up front, the more you owe at the end, due to compounding interest. If the value of your home declines, you will ultimately owe the lesser of the appraised value of the home or the amount of the outstanding loan. Finally, you don't make any payments until you move out for more than a year (say, to an assisted-living facility) or vacate the premises either to another location or to the hereafter.

Disadvantages: The major drawback is the high up-front costs. Lenders can charge an origination fee (which can be as much as 2 percent of the loan) and mortgage insurance, as well as fees for appraisal, document preparation, recordation, escrow, title insurance, and brokerage, which can add up to as much as $10,000 to $12,000 on a $300,000 reverse mortgage. In addition, these costs plus the monthly servicing and interest charges are all added to your outstanding loan. The result is that the amount owed grows over time, which, of course, is the reverse of paying off a traditional mortgage.

Further, interest rates can vary. You can get a fixed rate on a lump-sum distribution—great if rates are low. But if you decide to go the monthly installment or line-of-credit routes (which result in paying less interest than if you took the lump sum), the interest rate is variable. It's also worth noting that, if you decide to keep the home in the family, your kids will have to pay the loan off in full if they ever decide to sell the house. Finally, a reverse mortgage can adversely affect your eligibility for government assistance programs like Medicaid.

Line of Credit

Another way to tap into your home equity without all the costs and machinations of reverse mortgages is a home equity line of credit. This loan account would cost little or nothing to set up. But you should apply for this type of loan while you have a steady income, which will convince the lender that you are a good credit risk.

Keep in mind that, unlike the reverse mortgage, with a line-of-credit loan, you will need to make regular monthly payments. But it is certainly a better option than paying high interest rates on credit card balances.

Medicaid Waiver Program

Another way to afford to stay in your home is to qualify for the Medicaid waiver program. Although every state doesn't offer this alternative, those that do help pay for healthcare services in your home versus a nursing home. Covered services may include case management, homemaker services, home health aides, personal care, adult day programs, and respite care.

To qualify, you must meet the income and asset requirements in your state (which do not include the value of your home) and have a serious physical or mental condition. If you receive Medicaid services and you pass away, the state must try to recover the money it spent on your care from the estate.

Moving to Facilities Outside the Home

You should take the same disciplined, well-thought-out approach to moving to any type of assisted living as you did in considering the pros and cons of living in your home.

Further, by taking the initiative with your kids, whether it is for the traditional nursing home or the increasingly popular continuing care retirement communities, which include independent living, assisted living, and nursing care, you will be inoculating your family against an all-too-common and destructive confrontation: dragging Mom and Dad out of their home and into a nursing home for their own good (or is it for your own peace of mind?).

By involving your kids in the discussion, as well as arranging family field trips to nearby facilities, you will be able to see for yourselves some of the advantages: a common dining room; transportation alternatives; housekeeping; activities meant to relieve isolation, loneliness, and boredom; and à la carte services for evolving personal care and medical needs.

For nursing homes, you should begin your research phase by checking the quality ratings from independent sources like the federal government's Nursing Home Compare website at www.medicare.gov/nursinghomecompare.

Of course, when you make your actual on-site visits, you will want to go beyond just a look at the physical plant. Here are some things to look for:

- How do the staff approach their jobs?
- Does the place feel like it's the residents' home, or does it feel like a healthcare institution?
- Is it designed to make illness the center point of the residents' lives, or is it about life and living?
- Are there lots of activities offered, or is the television in the dayroom the main focus?

In other words, how much of the place is "nursing" and how much is "home"?

Living with Your Kids

Living with your kids not only offers less expensive independent living for your spouse and you, but it also can be a really positive experience for your entire family.

I remember spending my summers in a cottage in the middle of the woods in Michigan with my parents, brothers, and grandfather on my mother's side. Gramps, as we called him, brought a whole new dimension to my life, teaching me how to make a bow and arrow and how to track a deer, as well as regaling us all with tales of his growing up as a kid on the streets of London.

While living with your kids may sound good in the abstract, you will want the entire family to have a serious heart-to-heart discussion before you start packing your bags. Here are some questions that are designed to help you develop your own list of issues that you can lay out in the Other Talk:

- What will the financial arrangements be?
- How much will it cost to make any renovations along the lines that were covered in the "Living at Home" section earlier in this chapter?
- What are the kids' expectations of you regarding your helping them out with babysitting, grocery shopping, housekeeping, and so on?
- How will multiple cooks share the kitchen?
- How will you schedule time to sit down and share with one another how you think the arrangement is working out?
- How will you keep your marriage relationship a high priority in your lives?
- How can you remind your kids that they need to maintain the same priority with their spouses?
- How do your various children feel about your living with one of them?

- Should or could the living arrangement rotate among some or all of your children?
- What outside resources should you tap into for help in fulfilling your social needs and giving your kids a physical and psychological break from caregiving? How much will that cost?
- What happens if the arrangement doesn't work out?
- What happens if you become too sick or frail for your kids to handle? How will you as a group know that time has arrived?

Finally, whether this living arrangement is for you or not, I would suggest that you be careful how you approach this conversation with your kids. Several of my research respondents reported that their offspring were surprised and more than a little hurt when their parents declined to move in because they didn't want to be a burden, preferred being with people their own age, or didn't want to move away from their social network.

Living with Other People Your Age

A variation on living with your kids is sharing a house or an apartment with other friends your age. Not only do you share in the living costs rather than shouldering them yourself but you can also benefit on emotional, social, and even physical and psychological health dimensions.

As I recommended with the parents-and-kids arrangement, you will want to sit down with all the potential housemates to explore various aspects of this transaction:

- How will residents split the legal ownership, or title, of the home?
- How will the mortgage payment be divided along with other costs like taxes, insurance, utilities, and maintenance?
- Who will be responsible for the bill paying?
- Who gets to use what part of the house?
- What happens if one owner dies or needs to move?
- How and when will meals be prepared and shared?
- How will the shopping for food and other household tasks be assigned?
- What are the parameters for quiet time and social time?
- How will housemates resolve disputes?

Next Steps

We've just spent the last few pages discussing some of the living arrangements that you should consider as you enter your later years. But before we leave this subject, I want to make sure that I don't leave the impression that selecting the best living arrangement is a onetime, irrevocable decision.

In fact, I'd like you to consider your housing options much as I encouraged you to imagine your spending priorities in Chapter 7. The theoretical framework was by decade:

- Adventure travel in your sixties
- Guided tours in your seventies
- Theater and museum trips in your eighties
- Extreme bingo in your nineties

I would suggest that you think about your decisions regarding living arrangements to be equally fluid. I'd like you to set varying goals and priorities that are dependent on your physical abilities and your financial situation. And I would encourage you to include your kids in your thinking about these transition points because, as we all enter the inevitable world of role reversal, their involvement will only increase.

My grandma's journey in her last years may be instructive:

- In her seventies, her husband passed away, but she was comfortable living in her home, surrounded by her friends and her things.
- In her eighties, her brother died, leaving her a substantial inheritance. She decided to ditch home ownership (and responsibility) and find a residential retirement community and travel overseas (which she had never had the time or the means to do before).
- In her nineties, she moved to assisted living and enjoyed her friends, her family visits, and her daily soap operas.

CHAPTER NINE

Getting the Medical Care You Need

We need to remember as doctors that our job isn't just to cure. We also need to help navigate patients and families through a complex, chaotic time in their lives when they are disintegrating and their family may be disintegrating too.

—Dr. Greg Gramelspacher in the PBS documentary *On Our Own Terms*

Compared to past generations, we mature adults are healthier thanks to better nutrition, more attention to the importance of physical activity, and more and better medical procedures and medications to keep us going strong. We have a longer average life expectancy than our parents and grandparents too: 83.5 for men, 84.8 for women.

But just as your ability to enjoy life, liberty, and the pursuit of happiness will be unprecedented in your later years, so are the challenges that you will face in getting adequate medical care.

As I pointed out in Chapter 4, the rules of engagement will change in your last years:

- As you age, your need for resource-intensive healthcare will increase.
- The amount of public resources (such as Medicare and Medicaid) may look different than it does today.
- The availability of the traditional gatekeeper for your medical needs, the primary care physician, is dwindling.
- The number of elderly patients will increase exponentially, which will clearly put enormous strains on the current healthcare delivery system.

Therefore, if you expect to get the medical care you need, your family and you should start *now* to develop an assertive, proactive, thoroughly researched, well-designed strategy to ensure access to an increasingly complex and constrained medical care system.

As you develop your Other Talk approach to the unique medical challenges facing our generation, you should also keep in mind that it is already hard enough for many older Americans and their families to obtain the adequate healthcare.

Lack of Coordination

As you get older, chances are you will be treated by several different doctors, who may prescribe a variety of medications. The problem is that, for the vast majority of patients in the United States, there is no one medical practitioner who is charged with monitoring your condition or coordinating your various care providers. Here's how Dr. Gregg Warshaw, director of the Geriatric Medicine Program in the Department of Family and Community Medicine at the University of Cincinnati, in a 2007 *National Enquirer* article, described the situation:

> Individuals with three or four chronic illnesses have 8 to 14 physicians taking care of them. The complexity for caregivers is a tremendous challenge. Unfortunately, family physicians just aren't keeping track of all the specialists and medications a frail elder will need.

Problematic Access to Medical Care

Trying to make sense of this complexity and chaos, even if you are one of the top experts on medical care for the elderly, like Dr. Robert Kane, a researcher at the University of Minnesota, can leave you frustrated and angry. As reported in a National

Public Radio interview, Dr. Kane tried for a couple of years to care for his elderly mother, who had had a stroke. But despite all his expertise, he couldn't get things to work:

> Thirty years of practice and research wasn't worth a damn. . . . If somebody with my experience and my knowledge couldn't make the system work, what chance does the ordinary person who comes into this for the first time?
>
> I don't know how it's going to play out in the future. But I know right now we've got a mess on our hands. We have a system that, frankly, is broke and is costing us a lot of money, and it isn't producing the results that we really would like to see for ourselves or our parents.

Conflicting, Confusing Choices

I heard on numerous occasions during my focus groups with families that another extreme point of frustration is trying to make medical decisions for yourself or for a parent based on imperfect information.

Greta, the daughter of a Parkinson's patient, described her predicament this way:

> The doctor says to me, "This is the decision you have to make. I can't make that decision for you."

But if the doctor doesn't give you the information you need, how can he ever expect you to make a choice?

Colleen, with tears rolling down her cheeks, added her experience to the discussion:

In my mother's situation, there were two doctors on the team. One doctor said, "Don't take her off life support. She's got a chance."

The other doctor, in the same room, said, "Take her off. Nothing's going to help."

Well . . . what do I do?

Layers of Trauma for Your Kids

Your kids can become devastated in what can often be the cold, hard world of institutional medicine. This trauma is particularly likely if they are caught up in the middle of an unexpected parent care crisis without the preparation and discussion from the Other Talk. Dr. Jerald Winker, a practitioner of geriatric medicine for more than 30 years, paints this rather surreal picture:

The patient's family is already despondent, overwhelmed by Dad's (or Mom's) downhill progress and the acute event that brought him to the hospital (the pneumonia, the fall, the stroke); bewildered by his deteriorating course (the mental confusion, the weakness) while there and angered and frustrated in dealing with the bureaucracy (callous nurses, inattentive aides, even with the attending physicians who often drift quickly in and out on their rounds like white-coated apparitions).

Doctors' Hidden Agendas

In talking with a variety of medical practitioners and in researching the state of the profession, I was struck by the fact that the priorities that doctors bring to their practices don't always include the patient.

First, doctors—and particularly primary care physicians— are under increasing pressure from insurance companies and Medicare to build patient volume (which may be why fewer of today's medical students opt for primary care). This can be a particular problem for older patients, who may have more questions and need more detailed explanations. An internist in West Orange, New Jersey, one of my focus group participants, described it this way:

> My office visits are ludicrous: 15 minutes and you're out. But economically, just to keep the lights on, you have to see so many more patients than you should. You can't sit and talk.

A potential corollary to this economic burden is for doctors to recalibrate their practices based on profit margins.

Today, the same medical care is reimbursed at different rates, depending on whether the doctor sees a patient with private insurance, Medicare, or Medicaid. As demand increases relative to supply, which is the essence of my generation's perfect storm, some doctors will be motivated to accept only patients whose coverage pays the higher rates.

Another observation about the doctors' agenda, particularly in the last stages of life, is that doctors can become focused on cure at any cost because they are trained to fix things. Why would smart, intelligent, hardworking people be so committed (in some cases obsessed) with "cure at any cost"? It's not only because of the mindset established in medical school; it's also the amazing tools and techniques that they can now bring to bear.

Here's how Bernard, a social worker from my focus groups, characterized the situation:

What you've got are people who've always been the best of the best; they're very competitive to be successful; their goal is to always heal. . . . There are a lot of doctors out there where it's about them, and it's not about the patient and the family.

This single-minded focus on cure at any cost could be attributed to perceived pressures from the family. If the doctor starts to shift the conversation from cure to comfort (for example, to palliative and/or hospice care), the family and the patient might feel that "he or she has given up on me. It's the end. I've got nothing to look forward to. It's over!"

Rather than enter that confrontation, it may be easier for the doctor to continue looking for solutions because of the incredible tools that they have at their disposal. Dr. Nancy Kerr Akbari, an internist in Cambridge, Massachusetts, described the seduction of the medical toolbox this way in *On Our Own Terms*, a PBS documentary:

> New medical technology is great because there's pretty much always something that can be done. And I know from my experience that it's really hard to know when to stop.

Another aspect of this problem-solving mindset is that the physician often confuses treating the illness with treating the patient. Dr. Ken Brummel-Smith, chair of the Department of Geriatrics at the Florida State University College of Medicine, asserted on a panel discussion broadcast by NPR's *Talk of the Nation* in 2005, that the outcome can be ineffective, even counterproductive.

Unfortunately, our healthcare system is often oriented to diagnosis and intervention rather than enhancing people's functional level, their independence level.

Against this backdrop, I am heartened when I hear people like Leon Kass, a well-known physician and professor at the

University of Chicago, in a 2005 *Washington Post* article, take a much more profound look at the situation:

> We need to remember that old age and dying are not problems to be solved but human experiences to be faced.

In fact, this is a fundamental tenet of the Other Talk.

Don't Be Your Own Worst Enemy

The final obstacle to getting the medical care you need could be you. Unfortunately, the denial and procrastination that so many people cling to can be particularly dangerous when applied to medical treatment.

In a *Wall Street Journal* article, "Tackling the Emotional Side of Cancer," writer Amy Dockser Marcus introduces Yvette, a larynx cancer patient, as a real-life example of the risk of rejecting reality:

> Even when doctors told her that her prognosis was good, she said, "All I could hear was, 'You're going to die, you're going to die.'"
>
> So she broke doctors' appointments because she was frightened by seeing other patients there who had difficulty speaking because their voice boxes were removed during treatment.

Prepare Your Kids and Yourself to Become Medical Advocates

I am not laying out these obstacles—the perfect storm and the challenges of elder care—to scare or depress you. Rather, my goal is to inspire and motivate you to start the Other Talk process because gone are the days when you could passively depend on the doctor to take care of things.

If you are to get the medical care you need, you and your family will need to learn how to take control of your healthcare.

That means lining up the necessary resources before you need them, whether it's interviewing and selecting a geriatric doctor or geriatric care manager, visiting retirement facilities and senior activity centers, or exploring the extent of funding opportunities from Medicare, long-term care insurance, and beyond.

That means recognizing that the job of "medical advocate" is not only decision making on treatment options, living arrangements, living wills, etc. It is also coordinating various doctors and specialists, medical records, procedures, and current diagnoses, as well as negotiating with insurance companies, that are often the final arbiter over which treatment options will be covered.

That means that intimately involving your kids in your medical care not only lightens the load for you but it also provides teaching moments for them when the time comes for them to do battle as geriatric patients.

To achieve these objectives, I recommend that you incorporate the following seven-step checklist into your preparations for the Other Talk.

Step 1. Designate Your Medical Advocate

Talk with your spouse about which child (or children) would be the best candidate for your medical power of attorney. As you did for your financial power of attorney, you should establish selection criteria for this function as well. For example, Linda Kaare, the elder-law attorney in Michigan, suggests someone who is emotionally strong and courageous, curious and a good communicator, and willing to challenge the doctor in a productive manner.

As soon as your selected child has agreed to the responsibility and you have announced it to the family, you should sign the medical power of attorney document immediately. This is definitely a part of the Other Talk that you do not want to put off.

Step 2. Create Your Medical History

Update the medical section of the notebook that I discussed in Chapter 6, "Getting Your Documents in Order." You will want to make sure that your medical history documentation is current. Then, as time goes on, you should begin to chronicle your proactive resource explorations, including doctor interviews, retirement home visits, medical record keeping, and research into treatment options.

In addition, I would recommend that you build a medical family history for both your spouse and you. The purpose is to create an understanding of potential risk factors by linking family genes to predisposition for many chronic illnesses, like heart disease and various forms of cancer. The implication of these findings is not so you can live in fear and trepidation as you wait to be stricken by the "family curse." Rather, you can benefit on two levels:

- You can be proactive for conditions that are potentially preventable, including high blood pressure, heart disease, diabetes, depression, and alcoholism.
- You can be on the lookout for early symptoms of diseases included in your family history, and you can begin to learn about treatment alternatives and emerging medical breakthroughs.

According to a study published in the February 2012 issue of the *Annals of Internal Medicine*:

Detailed family information could help doctors better predict who is at risk and more accurately target patients for preventive care that may help avert the disease altogether.

It is also important to recognize when family ties don't increase the risk of getting a disease, as observed by Kelly Greene, the "Aging Well" columnist for the *Wall Street Journal*:

The genetic risk for Alzheimer's disease decreases dramatically between the ages of 60 and 85. . . . If you have a family member who contracted Alzheimer's after age 85, as many people do, there's little cause for worry.

In addition, I recommend that you review during your annual physical with your primary care physician or gerontologist all your medications and specialist treatments. Ask: Are they still effective in treating your current condition? Are they still necessary and cost effective?

Finally, I suggest that you explore the costs and benefits of routine screening for dementia because it is estimated that 8 percent of people over the age of 65 have some form of dementia, and that number doubles every five years over the age of 65. This screening was controversial in early 2012. The American College of Physicians, the U.S. Preventive Services Task Force, and the Alzheimer's Association discourage such regular monitoring, and they recommend that it be performed only if a patient reports a problem that could be due to dementia.

Step 3. Get the Most out of Your Doctor Visits

Take time to prepare for doctor visits with your child responsible for the medical power of attorney, whether he or she physically attends, participates via conference call or Skype, or is involved in phone calls before and after appointments.

To get the most out of the limited time you have with the doctor during an office visit, and to overcome the intimidation factor of the doctor's white coat, you should create a set of questions that prioritize your concerns. Here are some suggestions from the Agency for Healthcare Research and Quality website to get you started on your own list:

- What is my diagnosis?
- What are my treatment options? What are the benefits of each option? What are the side effects?
- Will I need a test? What is the test for? What will the results tell me?
- What will the medicine you are prescribing do? Are there any side effects?
- Why do I need surgery? Are there other ways to treat my condition? What is my post-surgical prognosis?
- How often do you perform this surgery?
- Do I need to change my daily routine?

No matter what questions appear on your list, you don't want to save your most important or embarrassing question for the end, when the appointment is almost over, with little time to address your most pressing concern.

Step 4. Prepare for Your Geriatric Care

As you near 65 and become eligible for Medicare, talk with your primary care physician about his or her willingness to take you on as a Medicare patient. This is an important conversation to have because doctor compensation is less with Medicare than with private insurance.

In preparation for your later years, you should also ask your doctor for recommendations and referrals for a geriatric care manager and a geriatric doctor.

A geriatric care manager brings to your care a working knowledge of health and psychology, human development, family dynamics, public and private resources, and funding sources that your kids and you can draw on. The function of the geriatric care manager is to plan and coordinate health and psychological care, along with "living issues" like house modifications, home care, socialization programs, and financial and legal planning.

A geriatric doctor is board certified in internal medicine or family practice, and he or she has undergone additional training to receive certification in geriatric medicine. The goal of this medical specialist is to prevent and treat diseases as they occur while also managing your eventual decline, helping you to maintain independence and to age as well as possible.

Step 5. Get Second Opinions

Seek out a second opinion when facing a major medical treatment, but be prepared for a potentially daunting task. Hospitals may put up major roadblocks because they see second opinions as time-consuming, distracting, and expensive. And doctors, especially specialists, may be resentful that their judgment is being questioned.

But second opinions are worth it nevertheless. In a 2002 Northwestern University School of Medicine review of 340 breast cancer patients seeking second opinions, reviewers disagreed with the first opinion 80 percent of the time, and they altered mastectomy or lumpectomy plans for 8 percent of the women, as reported in the *Annals of Surgical Oncology*.

Step 6. Incorporate Prevention into Your Healthcare Routine

Ensure that your medical care regimen includes an emphasis on preventive care, not just a focus on curing or treating an existing condition.

According to Daniel Perry, executive director of the Alliance for Aging Research, that doesn't always happen:

> Research shows that older patients aren't being steered toward the medical screening and preventive care they should get, even though Medicare would pay for much of it.
>
> There is a lot of withholding of aggressive treatment for people, based not on the evidence of whether they will benefit or not but by the perception of the physician that they're too old to benefit.

Judson, a 67-year-old Parkinson's patient who was in one of my focus groups, experienced this when pressing his specialist about a clinical trial for a new experimental drug.

The young doctor just looked at me and said, "Sir, you don't get it. There is only a limited supply of the drug available. They aren't going to waste it on you."

Step 7. Stay Current on Medical Innovations

Be vigilant in watching for developments that could have an impact on your health and well-being *and* help you stay afloat during my generation's perfect storm.

Certainly that means staying current on new drugs and surgical techniques that could improve or sustain your condition. But it also means looking for ways to enhance the delivery of your medical care.

Below are three examples of delivery innovations that, at this writing, are beginning to garner serious interest. While they may or may not fit your pocketbook, I hope you find them instructive.

Remote Monitoring

This technology enables doctors to check on patients who have chronic but easy-to-monitor diseases (for example, congestive heart failure, multiple sclerosis, and diabetes) without requiring a physical face-to-face interaction. It's a device installed in the home that monitors symptoms on the spot and sends a report to the doctor (and a family member, if desired) in real time. Benefits include fewer office visits, more productive and effective patient care, and a reduction in unnoticed complications that can result in hospitalization.

Patient-Centered Medical Home Model

This type of healthcare delivery system is currently being tested in a Medicare demonstration project and is part of the Affordable Care Act. The basic approach is for the primary care physician to take a more proactive role in your medical care, including managing and coordinating care; minimizing delays in getting appointments; partnering with patients with chronic diseases to manage their conditions and prevent avoidable complications; providing noncurrent medical advice via e-mail and phone; and offering a full spectrum of patient services from a team of healthcare professionals.

It almost sounds like my childhood family doctor, except he also made house calls.

Concierge Medicine

This type of medical practice, which initially emerged in the late 1990s, is based on greater attention from your primary care physician in return for an annual fee or retainer, which can generally vary widely from $200 to $2,000 per person, according to Forbes.com. Because doctors in a concierge practice see fewer patients than they would in a conventional practice, they often offer more leisurely office visits, are available by cell phone or e-mail, and will schedule appointments within days rather than months.

Navigating through the healthcare landscape during your last years of life will definitely be a challenge. But if your kids and you firmly commit to the advocacy approach to your medical care, I can assure you that your treatment outcomes will be better, your frustration level will be lower, and your children will be better schooled in managing their own healthcare.

Next Steps

As I've mentioned at several points in the book, the Other Talk should not be a onetime event but rather an ongoing update of changing conditions (financial and physical) as well as of documents, agreements, and shared responsibilities. Here's how I'd suggest you approach the medical care piece at your next Other Talk:

1. **Prepare a review of your current medical status.**
    I would encourage you to work on this update together with the child to whom you have given a medical power of attorney. This will build confidence and ownership of that role and ensure that you don't gloss over any unpleasant details.

    But it shouldn't be doom and gloom. Rather, "Here's the situation, and here's how we're going to deal with it."

2. **Review your medical care advocate options.** Since your medical condition will change and your kids' lives will evolve over time, I'd suggest you include two agenda items at your next Other Talk:

- Check on the continued availability and willing-ness of your current medical care advocate to do the job.
- Discuss with your spouse, then review with the family, a backup strategy in the event that the current medical care advocate can no longer perform.

This is in keeping with a basic premise of the Other Talk that developing what-if scenarios is much smarter than react-ing with panic to unexpected crises.

CHAPTER TEN

Taking Charge at the End of Your Life

I so wish my mother, who died of ovarian cancer, had done a living will. When she refused to eat, I was still fighting to save her through whatever artificial means the doctors could come up with. I'm so sorry I put her through that. It did not make her life one bit better.

—Suzie, focus group participant

How we die, the circumstances under which we die, what happens before we die, is under our control.

—Dr. Diane Meier, director of the Center to Advance Palliative Care at Mount Sinai in New York, in the PBS documentary *On Our Own Terms*

On the surface, this chapter heading could lead you to believe that my focus here is to help you ensure that decisions at the end of your life are made the way you want them to be. And, of course, that is my aim.

But I also want you to go beneath the surface and realize that in most cases, it is not about *you* taking charge at the end of your life. It's about you preparing and empowering *your kids* to take charge as you approach that final stage.

The reason for this collaborative approach is that it is highly likely that you won't be physically, emotionally, or mentally able to direct the final proceedings. It addresses the challenge for someone acting on your behalf to weigh the options and make decisions and to articulate what should be done in a way that reflects your thoughts about the end of your life.

This is a very real problem because, according to a 2003 Rand study, roughly 40 percent of deaths in the United States are preceded by a period of increasing frailty and often dementia lasting up to a decade.

As a result, it is critical that you start these conversations (as well as the rest of the Other Talk) *now*, while you are mentally sharp. Quite simply, the longer you wait, the less effective these discussions with your kids will be, due to the natural deterioration of the aging brain. Here's how Branch Rickey, the legendary baseball general manager in the 1920s through the 1950s, described that imperceptible evolution:

First, you forget names, then you forget faces, then you forget to zip your fly, then you forget to unzip your fly.

In preparing for the end game discussion in the Other Talk, you'll want to take steps in three critical areas: guiding principles, parameters for medical treatment, and hospice.

Step 1. Establish Your Guiding Principles

The first step in making your kids confident and empowered in taking charge when the time comes is for you to confront and define what "being alive" means to you as you near the end.

For some people, it is fighting for every last breath: "Even one more day would be important to me. I would do everything I could to hold on to life."

For others, it is living intensely, yet comfortably, in the time remaining: "I would rather be able to do what I want, to be with my kids, to enjoy life, even if it's for a shorter time."

Of course, neither one is the better approach because it is such a personal choice. But if you start now to build a clear understanding of your preferences with your family and your doctors, you can dramatically increase your odds of getting what you want.

Not surprisingly, coming to grips with what "being alive" means to you is easier said than done. My wife and I have found two online tools helpful in confronting this issue:

- **Five Wishes, developed by Aging with Dignity.** This booklet you fill out can help you articulate your feelings and opinions about the person whom you want to make care decisions for you when you can't; the kind of medical treatment you want or don't want; how comfortable you want to be; how you want people to treat you; and what you want your loved ones to know.
- **Proxy Quiz for Family or Physician, created by the American Bar Association (ABA) Commission on Law and Aging.** This document has 10 questions about your personal medical preferences, which your kids, your doctor, and you fill out separately. You then compare answers to find out where you need to correct the perceptions of your kids and your doctor on how you want to be treated at the end of your life.

One thing is certain: if you elect to procrastinate defining what "being alive" means to you and fail to empower your kids to carry out your own guiding principles, you will find yourself in the clutches of the medical profession's default position of treatment until cured (or dead).

There are a number of reasons for the medical profession's mindset.

Medical technology allows today's doctors to bring a dizzying array of medications and techniques to the table. Robert, one of my focus group participants with 10 years as director of medicine at a major Chicago hospital, painted this "because we can" scenario:

> There is always another layer of hope that we've created in medicine. We've got so many alternatives.
>
> If you don't have to pay for it and if there is no downside, you don't want Mom to miss an opportunity to continue living.

That's not always a good thing. A corollary to the power of technology is that it can cloud medical judgments. Victor, another one of my doctor participants, described the moral dilemma this way:

> Thanks to medicine's prowess in sustaining life, it is harder than ever to know when to stop.
>
> And because we as doctors are trained to "find the cure," we often forget to ask ourselves, "Is the illness getting the attention, or is the patient getting the attention?"

In addition to the medical advances, Medicare is set up to fund treatment until patients are cured. It's the reason that more than one-third of all Medicare spending is in the final year of life and one-sixth in the last month. As reported in a June 2009 article in *The Economist*:

The trouble with health care in America, says Muriel Gillick, a geriatrics expert at Harvard Medical School, is that people want to believe that "there is always a fix." She argues that the way Medicare is organized encourages too many interventions towards the end of life that may extend the patient's lifespan only slightly, if at all, and can cause unnecessary suffering. It would often be better, she thinks, not to try so hard to eke out a few more hours or weeks but to concentrate on quality of life.

We have been convinced by popular culture of the omnipotence of medical technology. In a 1996 study of a full season of medical shows like *ER*, 75 percent of patients who received CPR during cardiac arrest survived, and 67 percent recovered enough to leave the hospital. The reality is different, according to a February 2012 *Wall Street Journal* article: "a 2010 study of more than 95,000 cases of CPR found that only 8 percent of patients survived for more than a month. Of these, only 3 percent could return to a normal life." The upshot is that, while the doctor is busy trying to fix the problem, the patient as a human being can get lost in the shuffle. As one of my focus group participants, a doctor, observed:

We're prolonging life but we're also prolonging dying. Hundreds of thousands of people are surviving longer with advanced dementia or traumatic brain injuries or in coma states. In addition, for their loved ones, coping with the ambiguity of "not quite dead" creates a whole other level of stress.

Nadia, one of my participants, was born in Russia and was practicing medicine in the United States on a fellowship. She described her utter disbelief at how dying patients are treated in our society:

Everybody is treated until they are dead. Even if they are semi-dead, they are still treated. The patients are lying there at age 95, 96, 100, debilitated, demented, don't recognize anyone, don't eat [and] don't pee [on their own]. They're still treated.

Perhaps best capturing the emotional angst that can be visited on your kids by the medical community is Lester, 58, who is his dad's caregiver:

My father was at a very advanced stage of Alzheimer's. But the doctors kept hounding me. They would call me at work three or four times a week, telling me, "You shouldn't send him back to the nursing home. You should leave him in the hospital."

The fact is, the decision had been made a year ago with a healthcare power of attorney. It was very emotionally trying for me. I knew he was going to die shortly. But they made me feel bad by saying that if I took him out of the hospital, I would be the one who is causing his death.

Step 2. Set Parameters for Your Medical Treatment

Step 2 in taking charge of your life (versus abdicating it to the medical community) is to put your preferences in writing. Equally important is to distribute and discuss your wishes with your family members and your doctors to ensure that your goals will be achieved.

An effective and relatively inexpensive way to accomplish this is to consult with your legal advisor, then draw up a healthcare power of attorney.

This document establishes your designated agent who will make healthcare decisions for you if you are not able to do so. While rules can vary by state, typically responsibilities include the power to require, consent to, or withdraw any type of personal care or medical treatment and to admit you to or discharge you from any hospital, nursing home, or other institution.

A specific statement is included that allows you to address your opinion on life-sustaining treatment. For demonstration purposes only, here is the language for the three choices from the Illinois statutory short-form power of attorney for healthcare:

☐ I do not want my life to be prolonged, nor do I want life-sustaining treatment to be provided or continued if my agent believes the burdens of the treatment

outweigh the expected benefits. I want my agent to
consider the relief of suffering, the expense involved,
and the quality as well as the possible extension of
my life in making decisions concerning life-sustaining
treatment.

☐ I want my life to be prolonged, and I want life-sustaining
treatment to be provided or continued unless I am
in a coma that my attending physician believes to be
irreversible, in accordance with reasonable medical
standards at the time of reference. If and when I have
suffered irreversible coma, I want life-sustaining treatment to be withheld or discontinued.

☐ I want my life to be prolonged to the greatest extent
possible without regard to my condition, the chances I
have for recovery, or the cost of the procedures.

If you are in the "do not prolong life at any cost" camp,
you will also want to explore two healthcare directives: the
living will and the do-not-resuscitate (DNR) order:

- The **living will** establishes that you do not want your
death to be artificially postponed. It states that if your
attending physician determines that you have an incur-
able injury, disease, or illness, procedures that only
prolong the dying process should be withheld or with-
drawn, and only the administration of medication,
sustenance, or surgical treatments (as determined by

your attending physician) that provide comfort care should be used. This document must be signed by two witnesses who will not benefit from your death.

- The **do-not-resuscitate (DNR) order** is different from the healthcare power of attorney and the living will in that neither your healthcare agent nor you can prepare it. Rather, it is a written order signed by your physician that instructs other healthcare providers not to attempt CPR if your heart has stopped beating and if you have stopped breathing during cardiac or respiratory arrest.

  Since it is often relevant during an emergency situation, it is advisable to carry a DNR card and to distribute the document to family members and your doctors.

Once you have distributed your "what being alive means to me" documents (the healthcare power of attorney and, if relevant, the living will and the DNR order) and thoroughly discussed them during the Other Talk, your family and you should acknowledge the possibility of revisions. Every time your health status changes in some significant way, you should have another discussion to clarify your views and expectations.

It is okay for you to move the goalposts on issues pertaining to the end of your life. You just need to make certain that the people in your world know that you have moved them.

Step 3. Consider the Hospice Route

The final area for your consideration is to consider the pros and cons of hospice.

Hospice at the end of life isn't for everyone, and it certainly isn't for those who want to battle until their last breath. When you enter hospice—which you can often do either at home or in a facility—you agree to give up medical treatment. For you to qualify for Medicare coverage of hospice, at least one doctor must certify that you have six months or less to live and you have agreed to forgo life-prolonging treatments like dialysis, chemotherapy, and radiation.

The essence of hospice is that it isn't about perpetuating life; it is about perpetuating quality of life.

Conventional healthcare generally believes that when there is no possibility of recovery, the job is complete.

Hospice, on the other hand, believes that as long as a person continues to live, a great deal can be done to keep the patient as comfortable as possible, support the family as much as possible, and make the quality of life as fulfilling as possible, for as long as possible.

It achieves this by controlling a patient's pain and symptoms medically and, together with psychologists and social workers, by helping the patient grapple with depression, anxiety, fear, and spiritual issues. In addition, patients are encouraged to talk about feelings toward family members, regrets, and fences that may need to be mended.

Equally important, hospice treats family members as part of the plan for care.

Nurses visit once a week (or more frequently as needed), and they are on call 24/7 to respond to crises and questions on the phone or in person. Social workers visit as often as necessary to provide emotional support as well as to help find resources for wills, powers of attorney, funeral plans, and other needs. Home health aides assist with bathing, personal care, and homemaking to relieve family caregivers so they can take a break. Bereavement counselors provide care to the family for up to a year after the patient's death.

Jacques, one of my internist participants, painted the picture of hospice this way:

> It's about not suffering. It's about dignity and control and respect. It's about being able to go home, where you can just be comfortable with pain medicine and oxygen and not be in a hospital.

What may surprise you (as it certainly amazed me) is that hospice care doesn't shorten your life span, even though the hospice patient stops medical treatments and is permitted high-dose narcotics to combat pain. In fact, a study in the 2007 *Journal of Pain and Symptom Management* found that hospice patients lived 29 days longer on average than those who did not receive such services. As reported in the *New England Journal of Medicine,* a 2010 study of patients with advanced lung cancer who got palliative care along with standard cancer treatment found they had fewer symptoms of depression, received less chemotherapy, underwent fewer surgeries and other medical procedures, spent fewer days in the hospital, and lived 2.7 months (33 percent) longer that those who did not get those services. And hospice costs are usually covered all or in part by Medicare and private health insurance.

Here's a real-life example of how hospice can impact the final days, as told by Dr. Martha Twaddle, medical director of the Midwest Palliative & Hospice CareCenter:

This guy Marcus had a recurrent skin cancer that had gone back into his neck and wrapped around a carotid artery; there's nothing they can do.

So I walk in and say "Sir, how much do you know about your illness?" He's clueless. He's going to get married, he doesn't have a will, he has a major merger on the table with his board of directors.

So I say, "Sir, I'm going to be really straightforward with you. We don't have a lot of time here. Based on what's going on in your neck, I would estimate your life expectancy in terms of hours, if not days."

To his credit, he fit into the next seven days his will, his financial power of attorney, his wedding, and his negotiating instructions for the merger talks. Then he gave himself to hospice and quietly spent the next three weeks with his kids and his new wife.

How can hospice extend your life? Perhaps you live longer only when you stop trying to live longer. You are able to spend the remaining time at home, surrounded by your stuff, taking the opportunity to prepare yourself and your kids for the last sentence. You have an uninterrupted space to reminisce, talk about unresolved issues, and say your goodbyes to family and friends in a familiar, comfortable, pain-free setting.

Next Steps

We've come to the end of the action chapters so I want to leave you with a practical and a conceptual next step:

1. **Explore the reality of the do-not-resuscitate (DNR) order.** As I mentioned in Chapter 3, the Terry Schiavo case motivated my family to discuss the pros and cons of "extraordinary efforts to sustain life." If you recall, the four of us initially didn't agree on what my wife and I wanted done and not done toward the end of life, but we fixed it by putting it in writing.

   But my wife, Pam, and I soon realized that we needed to go further, that we needed to go beyond the hypothetical guessing what our personal preferences would be at the end. We needed to do a reality check of what actual conditions would trigger the DNR.

Here's what we did and here's what I would recommend to you:

- Schedule a meeting with your primary care doctor so that he or she can describe to your family and you the reality of conditions like late-stage cancer and dementia or severe brain damage.
- Establish with your doctor your personal trigger points for a DNR. You should also take this opportunity to fill out and discuss with your doctor a Physician Orders for Life-Sustaining Treatment (POLST) form. This document states what kind of medical treatment you'll want toward the end of your life. Because it is signed by both your doctor and you, a POLST enhances the control that seriously ill patients have over their end-of-life care. Every state in the United States has slightly different rules pertaining to a POLST, so I suggest you go to the Appendix, "Online Resources for the Other Talk," in this book to find relevant resources in your own state.
- If and when you suffer a life-threatening accident or illness, and assuming you are conscious

and lucid, meet again with your doctor and family to confirm your DNR instructions.

For my last recommended next step, I want you to step back from all the mechanics of financing your uncertain future, selecting the best living arrangements, getting the medical care you need, and taking charge at the end of your life.

2. **Remind yourself and make clear to your kids how the Other Talk will benefit them.** The Other Talk:

   - Teaches them to be flexible and adaptable as things change in unexpected ways
   - Empowers them to make the tough decisions if and when you can't
   - Gives them a template from which to discuss, explore, educate, and think about end-of-life issues with their own children
   - Demonstrates that "taking care of the kids after I'm gone" isn't just a financial issue
   - Adds a dimension to your family relationship that most kids will never know

CHAPTER ELEVEN

Being There for Your Kids

Fight to the end or depart comfortably?

It is one of the most important decisions you will ever make.

It is also one of the most courageous because you are taking the initiative to consider how you want to bring your life to a close.

Woody Allen once said, "I'm not afraid of dying. I just don't want to be there when it happens."

But because you have committed to having the Other Talk, you have decided that you *do* want to be there when it happens.

Because you want to be there for your kids.

On the surface, the Other Talk sounds like it is about being a great parent, about preparing your kids for one of life's great challenges. And it is.

But it also carries with it the added value of freeing you and your family to focus on getting the most out of the rest of your time together.

Finally, it helps ensure your family's well-being, financial and emotional, when you are gone.

In essence, the Other Talk will be an important part of your legacy.

Your kids will love you for it!

APPENDIX A

Sources

AARP

Aging with Dignity

American Bar Association Commission on Law and Aging

American Geriatrics Society

American Hospital Association

Annals of Internal Medicine

Bank of America

Employee Benefit Research Institute

Fidelity Investments

Gallup

Journal of the American Geriatrics Society

Journal of the American Medical Association

Medical Group Management Association

National Alliance for Caregiving

National Center for Health Statistics

Office of the New York State Comptroller

TIAA/CREF

U.S. Census Bureau

U.S. Centers for Disease Control and Prevention

APPENDIX B

Online Resources for the Other Talk

The resources that follow can help you develop your knowledge base, fill in your Other Talk notebooks (either paper or electronic) for each of your kids, and begin to explore your options for the four essentials of life I've talked about throughout this book:

1. Financing your uncertain future
2. Selecting the best living arrangements
3. Getting the medical care you need
4. Taking charge at the end of your life

I've listed in this Appendix a sampling of websites that are informative on these subjects. The list is organized around each of the action chapters, 5 through 10. The number of these sites, both for profit and not-for-profit, can be expected to grow as the interest in these subjects—particularly among people who are recently retired or soon will be and their families—mushrooms.

These resources can help you stay on top of your options, emerging medical treatments, and changing legal and financial regulations. Please note that, while some sites appear to be skewed toward adult children, the information and resources provided are relevant to all participants in the Other Talk, including the parents.

I would be interested in your feedback on the usefulness of these websites, as well as any additions you feel we should make. You can reach me at tim.prosch@theothertalk.com.

Chapter 5. Setting the Stage

AARP (www.aarp.org)

A nonprofit, nonpartisan organization that helps people 50 and older have independence, choice, and control in ways that are beneficial and affordable to them and society as a whole. AARP's website offers a great deal of consumer information, tools and worksheets, expert advice, online communities, and more.

Strength for Caring (www.strengthforcaring.com)

Provides access to others dealing with aging issues through "Share Your Story" and "Meet Other Caregivers" online bulletin boards.

Making the Decision to Stop Driving

AARP Driver Safety Program (www.aarp.org/driversafety)

Helps users recognize when it's time to limit or stop driving and how to discuss the issue with loved ones. Also provides a classroom and online course on up-to-date laws and safety measures to help adults keep driving.

American Automobile Association (SeniorDriving.aaa.com)

Provides information needed to continue driving, find transportation resources other than owning a car, and a self-test to see if you should still be driving.

Association for Driver Rehabilitation Specialists (www.driver-ed.org)

Helps you find a certified driving specialist who can help you determine whether it's time to give up driving, and it can also help you in retrofitting your vehicle if you have lost certain types of physical mobilities.

Beverly Foundation (www.beverlyfoundation.org)

Maintains a state-by-state list of programs providing transportation options for older adults.

Drivewise (drivewise.allstate.com)

The Drivewise device was initially created to provide data to insurance companies in order to give good drivers a discount. The device attaches to the car and records driving behavior for six months. It may tell you whether you should still be driving.

Independent Transportation Network (www.itnamerica.org)

   Provides a list of local affiliates that provide transportation for older adults. It also accepts donations of used cars for volunteers to drive seniors.

National Highway Traffic Safety Administration (www.nhtsa.gov)

   Provides a checklist to see whether you should still be driving (search for "driving safely while aging gracefully").

*Transportation for Seniors (*www.kued.org/productions/caregiving/pdf/30-a%20Community%20Transportation.pdf)

   Provides the "Community Transportation Resource Worksheet" to help you determine what transportation needs can be met by local community resources and public transportation.

Chapter 6. Getting Your Documents in Order

Where to Obtain Documents

Archives.com (www.archives.com)

   Provides copies of birth, death, marriage, and divorce records for a fee.

National Academy of Elder Law Attorneys (www.naela.org)

   Provides information on how and why an elder-law attorney can help in the areas of healthcare, retirement, tax, financial, estate, and Medicaid planning, and it offers a searchable database to find an elder-law attorney.

Sharing Your Information with Others

CareFlash (www.careflash.com)

Provides a system for creating and maintaining a private online calendar so that family, friends, and community members can determine how and when they can help.

eCare Diary (www.ecarediary.com)

Provides an online calendar so that family, friends, and community members can determine how and when they can help out. Also provides links for legal documents by state.

Lotsa Helping Hands (www.lotsahelpinghands.com)

Provides a tool where you can upload and share your schedule with family and friends and indicate areas where you need help. Also provides financial, legal, and medical documents, and hosts discussions with relevant experts.

Chapter 7. Financing Your Uncertain Future

Retirement Calculators

AARP as well as many investment firms, banks, and other nonprofit organizations provide online retirement planning computer models that help determine how long your money will last. The amount of detail and ability to personalize data vary greatly, but many calculators are surprisingly easy to use.

Money on About.com (www.Moneyover55.about.com/od/ preretirementplanning/a/retirementcalculators.htm)

Provides a review of online retirement calculators.

Sources of Additional Money

AARP (www.aarp.org)

Search "4 ways to tap your house for cash." Provides information on ways to get cash out of your home.

BenefitsCheckUp (www.benefitscheckup.org)

Many benefits go unused because people are not aware they qualify. BenefitsCheckUp provides an online survey to identify benefits that could help cover or lessen costs. The site creates a report detailing which programs could be beneficial in your situation and how to apply.

Five Best-Kept Secrets, Financing Senior Care & Assisted Living (www.aplaceformom.com)

Online pamphlet offers a wealth of ideas on financing care.

Five Ways to Cover Assisted-Living Expenses (www.bankrate.com/finance/insurance/paying-for -assisted-living-1.aspx)

Provides information on alternatives for covering assisted-living expenses.

National Association of Realtors (www.seniorsrealestate.com)

Lists local Realtors who specialize in selling homes of older Americans who are going through major lifestyle transitions.

National Center for Home Equity Conversion
(www.reverse.org)

Offers information on how you can get a reverse mortgage and use the proceeds for long-term care expenses, insurance premiums, or purchasing a less expensive primary residence. Also offers reverse mortgage counselors.

National Council on Aging Home Equity Advisor
(www.homeequityadvisor.org)

Provides information on reverse mortgages and consumer protections.

National Reverse Mortgage Lenders Association
(www.reversemortgage.org)

Offers information to help you determine whether a reverse mortgage is right for you.

Women's Institute for a Secure Retirement
(www.wiserwomen.org)

Provides information and tools to improve long-term financial security for women.

Money Management

American Association of Daily Money Managers
(www.aadmm.com)

Provides list of members who can assist with bill paying, banking, insurance paperwork, and organizing records in preparation for income tax filing, among other tasks.

Financial Planning Association (www.fpanet.org)

Provides a searchable database to help you find a financial planner.

National Academy of Elder Law Attorneys
(www.naela.org)

Provides information on how an elder-law attorney can help in the areas of healthcare, retirement, tax, financial, estate, and Medicaid planning, and it offers a searchable database to find an elder-law attorney.

National Association of Personal Financial Advisors
(www.napfa.org)

Includes a searchable database of fee-only financial advisors along with tips and techniques on financial planning.

National Council on Aging (www.ncoa.org)

Helps homeowners review their situation and explore options to boost their finances.

Frauds and Scams

AARP's Scams and Frauds page (www.aarp.org/money/scams-fraud)

Provides information about the latest frauds against older people.

Consumer Financial Protection Bureau's Office for Older Americans (www.consumerfinance.gov/older-americans)

Works to resolve consumer complaints specifically related to mortgages, credit cards, banks, loans, and more. Helps older Americans and their families with the financial challenges of aging.

Elder Financial Protection Network (www.bewiseonline.org)

Offers elder financial abuse prevention programs and community education events.

Federal Bureau of Investigation (www.fbi.gov/scams-safety/fraud/seniors)

Helps protect you and your family from fraud.

National Consumers League (www.natlconsumersleague.org)

Provides consumers with information about telemarketing and Internet fraud.

National Do Not Call Registry (www.donotcall.gov)

Placing your telephone number on this list will stop most telemarketing calls.

North American Securities Administrators Association (www.nasaa.org/investor-education)

Provides tools and techniques on what to watch for and what to do if you think you are being scammed by financial advisors.

"Protecting Mom & Dad's Money: What to Do When You Suspect Financial Abuse," Consumer Reports magazine, January 2013.

An excellent article that features ways to protect yourself from financial abuse, including abuse from your own relatives.

Elder Abuse

National Adult Protective Services Association (www.napsa-now.org)

Provides a list of state protective services agencies that handle elder abuse cases.

National Center on Elder Abuse (www.ncea.aoa.gov)

Search the frequently asked questions (FAQ) to look at various scenarios and what to do about them.

National Long-Term Care Ombudsman Resource Center (www.ltcombudsman.org)

Advocates for residents of nursing homes, board and care homes, and assisted-living facilities, and can report suspected abuse.

Chapter 8. Selecting the Best Living Arrangement

Finding a Provider

A Place for Mom (www.aplaceformom.com)

A Place for Mom will put you in touch immediately with a free personal consultant who is well versed in the retirement, continuing care, assisted-living, and nursing homes available in your community.

Caring.com (www.caring.com)

Provides information and a searchable database of living options with candid reviews from residents and people who have visited the facilities or used its services. Types of services listed include the following:

- Adult Daycare
- Alzheimer's Care Facilities
- Area Agencies on Aging
- Assisted-Living Facilities
- Continuing Care Facilities
- Elder Law Attorneys
- Geriatric Care Managers
- Government Health Insurance Counselors
- Home Health Agencies
- Hospice Agencies
- Independent Living
- In-home Care
- Nursing Homes
- Senior Home Remodeling Services
- Senior Move Managers

LeadingAge (www.leadingage.org/findmember.aspx)

Provides a searchable database of nursing homes, home healthcare providers, hospitals, and community services for older Americans; does not provide comparisons.

Medicare (www.medicare.gov/nhcompare)

Provides a searchable database that compares nursing homes, home healthcare providers, and hospitals in your area.

National Alliance for Caregiving (www.caregiving.org)

Provides a clearinghouse of resources that have been reviewed and rated.

National Care Planning Council (www.longtermcarelink.net)

Offers links to all types of care services for older adults and a directory to find local organizations.

Living at Home

American Society of Interior Designers (www.asid.org)

Provides information about "universal design"—buildings, products, and environments that are accessible to residents of all ages and abilities.

Center for Aging Services Technologies (www.agingtech.org)

Provides information on technology to improve the lives of older adults, including a video on aging-in-place technology.

Center for Universal Design (www.design.ncsu.edu/cud)

Offers information about improving accessibility in your home.

Eldercare Locator (www.eldercare.gov)

Helps you find government services and programs in your area for older adults and their families.

Empowering Parents (www.empoweringparents.com)

    Provides ideas and rules for living with adult children in their home or yours.

MealCall (www.mealcall.org)

    Lists local providers of meal programs at locations in your community.

Meals on Wheels Association of America (www.mowaa.org)

    Lists local providers of nutritious prepared meals that can be delivered to your home.

National Adult Day Services Association (www.nadsa.org)

    Provides information on how to choose an adult daycare center and a database to help find a center in your area.

National Aging in Place Council (www.ageinplace.org)

    Provides a searchable database of service providers, including financial and caregiving options, that can help you stay in your home.

National Association of Area Agencies on Aging (www.n4a.org)

    Offers a searchable database of state and local chapters that provide a variety of supportive services, including help with household chores, meals served in community locations, adult daycare programs, protective services, and legal counseling.

National Resource Center on Supportive Housing and Home Modification (www.homemods.org)

Offers a searchable database of hundreds of local resources for home modification, tips on how to assess your home safety, and information about funding sources for home modification. The center does not endorse or qualify service providers.

Program of All-inclusive Care for the Elderly (PACE) (www.pace4you.org)

Provides a searchable database to find a local Program of All-inclusive Care for the Elderly (PACE). Provides one-stop shopping for all the services you might need to remain in your home. Not available in all states.

Living with Your Children

Family Education (www.familyeducation.org)

Search for "living with your adult children." Provides advice for living with your adult children.

Voices.yahoo (http://voices.yahoo.com/senior-tips-living -adult-child-121843.html)

Offers tips for older adults living with their children.

Living with Others

Aging in Community (www.agingincommunity.com/models)

Provides links to a growing number of groups that offer a support structure to help older adults stay in their homes. These "villages" also provide events and get-togethers for their members.

Assisted-Living Communities

Assisted Living Federation of America (www.alfa.org)

Lists assisted-living communities in your local area and provides a checklist to help you assess services, amenities, and accommodations.

Hospitals

Hospital Compare (www.medicare.gov/hospitalcompare)

Helps you compare hospitals in your area.

Chapter 9. Getting the Medical Care You Need

Caregiving

AARP Caregiving Resource Center (www.aarp.org/caregiving)

Provides tools and tips on how to succeed as a caregiver, including a care provider locator and an online community.

AARP Guide to Caregiving (www.aarp.org/guidetocaregiving)

E-book addressing all aspects of caregiving, from health, housing, and legal matters to ways to handle the emotional transitions, where to find support, and how to care for the caregiver. In English and Spanish.

Family Caregiver Alliance (www.caregiver.org)

Offers information on caring for a loved one, including a handbook for long-distance caregivers. Use the Family Care Navigator to find caregiver resources for your state.

Knowing Your Medical Rights

Medicare Rights Center (www.medicarerights.org)

Offers services to help Medicare recipients and their caretakers learn and understand the options and sources available to them.

National Association of Professional Geriatric Care Managers (www.caremanager.org)

Lists geriatric care managers in your local community and explains the duties and responsibilities of a geriatric care manager.

Patient Advocate Foundation (www.patientadvocate.org)

Helps you learn how to appeal insurance company denials of coverage and discrimination because of an illness.

Disease Information

Alzheimer's Association (www.alz.org)

Offers information about the medical and emotional issues surrounding Alzheimer's disease.

American Cancer Society (www.cancer.org)

Provides information about the medical and emotional issues surrounding cancer.

American Diabetes Association (www.diabetes.org)

Offers information about the medical and emotional issues surrounding diabetes.

American Heart Association (www.heart.org)

Offers details about the medical and emotional issues surrounding heart conditions.

American Lung Association (www.lung.org)

Offers information about the medical and emotional issues surrounding lung diseases such as chronic obstructive pulmonary disease (COPD), emphysema, chronic bronchitis, asthma, and lung cancer.

Healthinaging.org (www.healthinaging.org)

Provides health information about diseases that are prevalent in older adults.

Leukemia & Lymphoma Society (www.lls.org)

Provides information about the medical and emotional issues surrounding leukemia and lymphoma.

National Comprehensive Cancer Network (www.nccn.com)

Offers guidance on how to cope with distress, including meditating, keeping a journal, joining a support group, and creating a support team of family and friends.

National Institute on Aging (www.nia.nih.gov)

Provides information on health topics as you age, including information on Alzheimer's disease.

National Kidney Foundation (www.kidney.org)

Offers information about the medical and emotional issues surrounding kidney disease.

Parkinson's Disease Foundation (www.pdf.org)

Offers information about the medical and emotional issues surrounding Parkinson's disease.

Medications

American Society of Consultant Pharmacists (www.ascp.com)

Lists local senior care pharmacists who can help you manage your medications.

National Council on Patient Information and Education (www.talkaboutrx.org)

Provides information on the appropriate use of your medications, how they might affect you as you age, and how to better manage them.

Chapter 10. Taking Charge at the End of Your Life

Advance Directives

aarp.org/advancedirectives

Provides state-by-state forms and instructions for advance directives.

Advance Directive Health Care Card (www.aha.org/putitinwriting)

Provides a wallet card to alert healthcare workers that patients have talked to their family about advance directives and how to contact relatives.

Aging with Dignity (www.agingwithdignity.org)

Contains the Five Wishes document, which helps you express how you want to be treated if you are seriously ill and unable to speak for yourself.

American Bar Association Commission on Law and Aging (www.americanbar.org)

Offers the "Consumer's Toolkit for Health Care Advance Planning." Includes easy-to-use, self-help worksheets that can help you determine your long-term wishes and who might be best to help carry out your decisions. Tool #7 offers a quiz for your families and doctors to determine your wishes for medical treatment toward the end of life.

Eldercare Mediators (www.eldercaremediators.com)

Offers information on how eldercare mediators can help resolve conflicts among loved ones without advocating for one particular party.

Islamic Medical Association of North America (www.imana.org)

Provides a living will and advance directive that balance Islamic prohibitions against suicide with the desire to not prolong life at all costs.

Physician Orders for Life-Sustaining Treatment (POLST) Paradigm (www.polst.org)

Provides information including a video on what POLST is, why it is needed, and how it complements but does not replace an advance directive. Information is provided on a state-by-state basis.

The Conversation Project (www.theconversationproject.org)

Provides a starter kit to help begin end-of-life conversations with loved ones.

Hospice Agencies

Americans for Better Care of the Dying (www.abcd-caring.org)

Provides information about end-of-life issues, including the aptly titled *Handbook for Mortals*.

Caring Connections (www.caringinfo.org)

Provides information about end-of-life issues, including information about hospice and palliative care and how to find options in your community.

Hospice Foundation of America (www.hospicefoundation.org)

Offers information about the hospice concept of care, as well as suggestions for dealing with grief in workplaces, schools, and places of worship.

National Association for Home Care & Hospice (www.nahc.org)

Offers a searchable database to find local home care and hospice agencies.

National Hospice and Palliative Care Organization (www.nhpco.org)

Offers information on end-of-life issues and a searchable database of providers.

National Institute for Jewish Hospice (www.nijh.org)

Provides information about specific issues surrounding hospice for those of the Jewish faith and lists of accredited Jewish hospice organizations.

Funerals

Funeral Consumers Alliance (www.funerals.org)

Provides information from an independent source on how to plan a funeral, make sure that your legal rights as a consumer are respected, and plan a green burial.

National Funeral Directors Association (www.nfda.org)

Provides information on traditional funerals, cremation, and dealing with grief.

Tools and Tips for the Other Talk

To help you organize all the information and documentation that you will want to include in your Other Talk notebooks (whether they are electronic folders or physical binders), I have created the following worksheets that you can adapt to focus your efforts.

My goal here is to lay out the task in bite-size pieces for each of the action chapters rather than present you with one large, overwhelming project.

Whether you decide to divvy up specific assignments by family member or do them all yourself, this Appendix will give you a running checklist on the issues, information, and discussions that you are ready for and those that you still need to work on.

Finally, please keep uppermost in your mind that the Other Talk is about enhancing relationships and sharing responsibilities with your kids. It is not just an exercise in collecting paperwork for a notebook.

Chapter 5. Setting the Stage

Start with Your Commitment to the Philosophy of the Other Talk

- Acknowledge the inevitability of ceding to your kids the decision making and management of your day-to-day responsibilities.
- Establish ground rules on the trigger points that will effect the change of responsibilities in key functions, such as bill paying, transportation, living arrangements, money and asset management, and medical decisions.
- Realize that your plan for role reversal is not about the loss of power and control. Rather, it is about the gain of security and freedom.
- Incorporate full financial disclosure into the partnership with your kids.

Prepare Your Kids Emotionally and Psychologically

- Consider giving each of your kids a copy of this book before you sit down to have the Other Talk.
- Encourage your kids to adopt the collaborative mindset inherent in the Other Talk with their siblings and you.
- Establish that the Other Talk is an ongoing annual conversation, not a onetime event, to allow the family to deal with changes in your physical, mental, and financial condition as well as external factors (such as medical breakthroughs and government policy revisions).

- Spend time creating a welcoming and engaging environment for the Other Talk.

Chapter 6. Getting Your Documents in Order

In preparation for the Other Talk, you need to collate and organize binders (either electronic or paper) for each of your kids that will not only give them a working knowledge of your situation and your philosophies but also will house a knowledge base that can be updated as time goes on.

Will or Trust

- Location of original document
- Date last revised

Medical Information

- Copies of advance directives (healthcare power of attorney, living will, and DNR)
- Information on doctors
  - Name and contact information
  - Medical specialty
  - Brief description of diagnosis
  - Treatment plan and timeline
- Summary of medications
  - Type and strength of prescription
  - What the medication is treating
  - Location for prescription refills (pharmacy or mail order)
  - Name of physician who wrote the prescription

Financial Information

- Contact information for key advisors (attorney, financial planner, accountant, stockbroker, real estate agent, and others) including name, address, phone and fax numbers, and e-mail addresses

Key Documents

- Location of the following original documents
  - Birth certificate
  - Social Security card
  - Marriage certificate
  - Divorce judgment and decree, or the stipulation agreement if settled out of court
  - Passport
  - Trust documents

Insurance for Life, Health, Homes, Vehicles, and Boats

- For each policy
  - Name of carrier
  - Policy number
  - Policy type
  - Name of agent connected to the policy

Location of Your Most Recent Seven Years of Tax Returns

Bank Accounts and Safety Deposit Boxes for All Checking and Savings Accounts

- Location
- Account numbers

- Names on accounts
- Contact information
- Passwords
- For safety deposit boxes
  - Location
  - Contents
  - Location of keys

Proofs of Ownership

- Location of original documents
  - Housing and land ownership deeds
  - Cemetery plots
  - Vehicle and boat titles
  - Savings bonds
  - Partnership or corporate operating agreements

Location of Investment, Pension, and Loan Information

- Inventory of current investments, including traditional and Roth IRA accounts and 401(k) and 403(b) plans
  - Account numbers
  - Contact information for who handles each
  - Passwords
- Most recent statement from Social Security
- Original mortgage and any home equity loans and most recent refinancing details
- Summary of loans you have outstanding and the repayment terms
- Summary of debts you owe

Credit Card Information

- Location of most recent statement
- Front and back copies of all active credit cards
- Passwords for accessing accounts

Burial and Funeral Information

- Summary of your wishes
  - Cremation or burial
  - Type of service (where, what kind, visitation, specific music and/or readings, military proceedings, etc.)
  - Organ donation arrangements and time frame
  - Location of burial plot, type of grave marker
  - Charity donation (in lieu of flowers)
  - Prepaid funeral and/or burial insurance policy, with name of carrier, agent, policy number, and the policy type and specifics

Chapter 7. Financing Your Uncertain Future

- Frame your spending priorities by answering the questions: What is the life you want? What is the life you don't want? What are the costs of each?
- Establish goals and priorities by decade: sixties, seventies, eighties, and nineties.
- Develop a retirement income plan, which will require you to accumulate the following information:
  - Annual expenses
  - Essential expenses

- Discretionary expenses (for example, travel, entertainment, and clothes)
- Supplemental healthcare insurance
- Long-term healthcare insurance
- Income
- Social Security benefits and start dates for husband and for wife
- Pension benefits
- Annuity income
- Other income (such as dividends, interest, rental income, real estate sales including your home)
- Current assets
- Investment portfolio, including the dollar amount and percentage of total for stocks, bonds, and short-term instruments
- Real estate and other assets (such as antiques and artwork)
- Level of risk you are comfortable with
- Answer key decisions in your retirement plan (free financial planning software programs can be helpful):
  - How long will you and your spouse live?
  - Can your investment portfolio at least match the rate of inflation?
  - Have you established a withdrawal rate that won't jeopardize your long-term future?
  - Have you set aside funds to supplement Medicare and cover out-of-pocket healthcare costs?

- Do you want to leave an inheritance for your kids and others as well as donations to charity, or do you plan to spend it all?
- Establish a financial power of attorney with one of your kids.
- Schedule time for you and all of your kids to sit down for face-to-face meetings with any financial advisors you might have (bankers, lawyers, brokers, accountants, insurance agents, financial planners, and so on).
- Prepare now for potentially shifting financial roles between you and your spouse.

Chapter 8. Selecting the Best Living Arrangement

In preparation for the Other Talk, thoroughly discuss with your spouse where you want to live in your last years and how that can be accomplished. Look at these options:

- Living at home until the very end
- Moving to some form of assisted-living facility
- Living with your kids
- A combination of all of the above

Living at Home Until the Very End

- Consider the need for help with everyday tasks, more frequent access to healthcare providers, and the potential for loneliness and isolation as well as the various costs of home ownership.

- Prepare to modify your home to maximize comfort, accessibility, and safety.
- Start now to educate yourself and your family about assisted-living at-home alternatives.
- Explore funding opportunities as a homeowner including reverse mortgages, lines of credit, and the Medicaid waiver program.

Moving to Some Form of an Assisted-Living Facility

- Arrange family field trips to nearby facilities to evaluate the pros, cons, and costs of various alternatives.
- Evaluate each facility to determine how much of the place is "nursing" and how much is "home."

Living with Your Kids

- Initiate a serious heart-to-heart discussion on the various emotional, physical, and financial implications.

Chapter 9. Getting the Medical Care You Need

Recognize that obtaining quality healthcare as a geriatric patient will likely be more complicated, confusing, and frustrating than it was to get care when you were younger.

As you sail into the baby boomers' perfect storm, prepare yourself and your kids to become medical advocates by taking the following steps:

- Designate one of your kids as medical power of attorney.

- Ensure that your medical history documentation is current and comprehensive.
- Take time to prepare for doctor visits with your child who is responsible for the medical power of attorney.
- Discuss with your doctor how your relationship may change once you become eligible for Medicare.

Chapter 10. Taking Charge at the End of Your Life

Establish guiding principles with your family and doctors:

- Define what "being alive" means to you.
- Consider using tools to help you and your kids get through this most difficult of conversations (such as the Five Wishes or the Proxy Quiz for Family or Physician).
- Set your parameters for end-of-life medical treatment, and include a medical power of attorney, living will, and do-not-resuscitate (DNR) order, if appropriate.
- Consider the pros and cons of hospice.

Index

About the Author

Tim Prosch is president of the marketing firm Contact Points, Ltd. He previously taught at Northwestern's Kellogg School of Marketing. Prosch and his work have been featured in the *Wall Street Journal* and *USA Today* as well as on CNBC.